D1440896

Mysteries of the Rosary in Ordinary Life

Teresa Rhodes McGee

ORBIS BOOKS
Maryknoll, New York 10545

The Catholic Foreign Mission Society of America (Maryknoll) recruits and trains people for overseas missionary service. Through Orbis Books, Maryknoll aims to foster the international dialogue that is essential to mission. The books published, however, reflect the opinions of their authors and are not meant to represent the official position of the Society. To obtain more information about Maryknoll and Orbis Books, please visit our website at www.maryknoll.org.

Copyright © 2007 by Teresa Rhodes McGee.

Published by Orbis Books, Maryknoll, New York, U.S.A.

Manufactured in the United States of America.

Library of Congress Cataloging-in-Publication Data

McGee, Teresa Rhodes.
  Mysteries of the rosary in ordinary life / Teresa Rhodes McGee.
    p. cm.
  ISBN 978-1-57075-699-3 (pbk.)
  1. Rosary. I. Title.
  BX2163.M34 2007
  242'.74—dc22
                          2006038138

To my mother,
Kathleen Kennedy Rhodes,
whose fidelity to the rosary has circled the earth

CONTENTS

CONTENTS

The Sorrowful Mysteries

The Glorious Mysteries

INTRODUCTION

It was a steamy afternoon in Manhattan. I made my way through Grand Central Station wearing the same unyielding look of determination that was on the faces of all of the other irritable people who just wanted to go home. The station was crowded and hot. Every single person in the rush-hour crowd was intent on making a train. I dodged in and out of the crowd and jumped on my train just before it started to move. Falling into the first available seat, I sighed and uttered that most worn of lines—"Can you believe how hot it is?"—to the woman sitting next to me. I then reached into my briefcase for a book and wearily began to read. The woman beside me pulled a glass beaded rosary from her pocketbook, kissed the cross, closed her eyes, and silently began to pray.

The tender movement of her fingers over the beads caught my attention and soothed my own spirit. I could see out of the corner of one eye the woman's fingers passing silently through the mysteries of Christ; out of the corner of the other eye I saw the Hudson River flowing steadily. Both the river and the rosary were gentle reminders of baptism into a source of life much deeper than I can see or imagine. In a most unexpected way, a stranger called me to the thanksgiving of evening prayers counted out on one's fingers.

Repetition of the rosary prayers deepens reflection on the sacred mysteries of God's relationship with us. When we pray the rosary, we recall that we are joined with God in the unfolding story of redemption. Since its beginnings in the eighth century, praying the rosary has been connected with scripture both as a psalter and as a way of telling the gospel story. Each bead recalls a psalm, each mystery reveals something of Jesus Christ. Praying the rosary makes the gospel story accessible to everyone hungry for a daily connection to faith, regardless of their level of education. That accessibility of the holy has made the rosary a form of prayer offered as often in kitchens, on trains, and at the bedside of a sick child as it is in cathedrals. It is a prayer of life as close as our memories and fingers, an immediacy that reflects God's presence among us as our lives unfold.

Pope John Paul II, in a pastoral letter written in October 2002, called us to integrate the mysteries of Jesus' public ministry into our rosary prayers, and named five events, which he called the "luminous" mysteries or the "mysteries of light." These mysteries are rooted in the life of Jesus from his baptism to his gift of the Eucharist. "Certainly the whole mystery of Christ is a mystery of light," wrote John Paul II. "He is the light of the world

(John 8:12). The truth emerges in a special way during the years of Jesus' public ministry." Praying and reflecting on the luminous mysteries gives us deeper knowledge of the light of Christ in our own lives.

What we tend to think of as the rosary—five decades, each reflecting on a mystery—is really only one fourth of a rosary. To say the entire rosary is to pray all of the mysteries through the repetition of the prayers; twenty decades offered over time—annunciation through crucifixion through the crowning of Christ's mother in heaven and on earth. Together, the mysteries of the rosary celebrate the unbroken circle of God's loving relationship with us in the joyous, luminous, sorrowful, and glorious mysteries of our day-to-day lives.

Whether prayed in a spirit of supplication, praise, petition, or simple exhaustion, the rosary never strays far from the events of the day. We know deep within us the mysteries these prayers evoke. As we move our fingers along the beads, the mysteries of our own lives find redemptive expression in the mysteries of the rosary. The rosary is about the relationship between God and humanity; it is about mother and child, divine mysteries flowing through our veins in a transformative journey that takes us to Bethlehem, Cana, Calvary, Pentecost, and the promise of eternal life. Each of the mysteries reveals something specific about a relationship with God that is as certain and as palpable as the love between Jesus and the woman who gave him birth.

Praying the rosary honors the mysteries of our lives, for each of us knows moments of annunciation and visitation; crowning with thorns and with glory; and limitless opportunities to cry out of a sense of abandonment by God. We carry these experiences and stories with us like rosary beads in our pockets; they are comforting, they are challenging, they are a call to prayer. Each of these stories brings us to a place of knowing more intimately the divine mysteries repeated and revealed in the experience of human life.

This book is a meditation on those eternal mysteries lived in contemporary flesh. It is a series of twenty stories that reflect the way in which the events of Mary and Jesus' lives intersect our own experience, focus our prayers, and renew our hearts. Each story flows from the themes of one of the mysteries of the rosary and represents moments in life that lead us to reach for God. Each story is its own meditation on a mystery and is, as such, a point of entry into the entire story of God's loving revelation.

The stories have within them a quiet echo that is the sound of our ancestors praying their beads and finding peace. These reflections are to be read as an invitation to pray in an ancient circle that joins our own life mysteries with the incomprehensible mystery—and mercy—of God. They are, at heart, stories of blessed fruit given from God's own womb.

The Joyful Mysteries

THE ANNUNCIATION

"You see before you the Lord's servant,
let it happen to me as you have said."
(Luke 1:38)

Many years have passed since I was in Lima, since I met Sylvia, since her annunciation in the desert sand. Everything about her remains fixed in my memory like a Wisdom passage that I must grow into understanding.

Sylvia lived with her husband and children in one of Lima's new towns, a settlement stretching upward from a coastal desert to the Andean foothills. The original settlement had begun thirty years earlier when, on Christmas Eve, thirty thousand people had staked a claim on abandoned land with renewed hope that the desert could be fertile. Carrying straw mats and all that they owned, the people built shacks on the land that, over time, became solid buildings.

The government referred to the new settlement as an "invasion." A newspaper writer described the new settlement as "Ciudad de Dios—City of God." The name and all of its meanings became permanent.

Like her neighbors, Sylvia built her house one brick at a time over a period of many years. Each of its bricks represented struggle, tenacity, and courage at a time when bricks and mortar were as precious as gold. Sylvia's solid house had foundations deeper than the difficult sands of Lima's desert. She lived in the City of God, and God dwelled with her. God always beckoned, and Sylvia provided hospitality in the sanctuary of her house and her heart, dwelling places formed by struggle and hope.

"I talk to God when I am cooking," she once told me. "My children ask me who I am speaking with and I tell them I am talking to God. They say, 'God is by our stove?' and I say, 'Of course. God lives in our house. God lives here with us.' And they ask me where, and I tell them 'everywhere.' I don't think they understand, but I know someday they will."

In my own way, I had as much difficulty understanding Sylvia's proclamation of faith as her own children did. I was ashamed to discover within myself such an attachment to external circumstances, so many lingering illusions that Jesus is born only in the most beautiful of places. Sylvia knew herself to be a carrier of God in the most intimate and tender places of her life— places that to me, in my blindness, seemed too stark to be blessed. Sylvia's fertility in the desert went much deeper than outward appearances; it was founded on the knowledge that no house is too humble, no body too broken to bear God's life in the world.

I knew and prayed the annunciation from a place of comfort and certain knowledge of how the story works out. The visions of angels and Mary with a halo already in place had skewed my perception. Somehow I had come to believe that Mary's call to be the Mother of God had unfolded in a context of absolute security and gilded beauty.

Sylvia challenged me to see that all around us is the expectancy of the Word made flesh. Each one of us is called to bring the life of Jesus into the world. Sylvia knew experientially what my protected perspectives had missed: all hospitable hearts and houses—especially small houses courageously built on desert sand—are wombs for the living God.

When I am in a receptive space, Sylvia still speaks to me. She reminds me that God is with me in my kitchen, in my house, in the womb of my life. The reminder comes at times when I least expect it and often when I least believe that I am capable of bringing God into the world. Sylvia speaks across years that have brought great joy—children, growth, the deepening of roots— and great challenges.

For several years, chronic illness has been the desert on which my life is built. I suffer from aggressive rheumatoid arthritis, a painful and exhausting ailment controlled by equally exhausting medications. The systemic disease works its way into my body's tiniest cells so insidiously that—without my permission—it has prematurely ended my childbearing years and occasionally leaves my spirit as barren as stone. Sometimes it feels as though I have been sick longer than I was well.

Ongoing illness has a way of distorting time, diverting attention, and rearranging the spirit. It is tempting to forget what came before the illness, because the memory of health can create more of a sense of loss than of comfort.

When a fragile, brokered peace exists in my body, as it does right now, I must be careful to preserve my energy and remain faithful to my medication. I cannot use the spaces of reduced pain as an opportunity to "catch up on living." Rather, such moments are a gift that strengthens my spirit for times when the pain is relentless. When such times come, it is easy to lose the memory and vision of health, to believe that the struggle of each day is all that there is, and, God forbid, to give into the isolating nature of pain. It is sometimes all too easy to believe that divine fertility is only for the strong or that bringing life into the world depends on the power of my own efforts.

At moments like these, Sylvia's wisdom beckons and I find myself answering her in real time, "Yes, God lives in my house." The annunciation of Christ's birth unfolds in the real space and time of a profoundly broken world. I have come to know this brokenness in my own body. Chronic disease has taught me to think of life in less objective, stratified terms. It has taught me that the journey of faith is not neat and clear, predetermined, or known in advance. In this day, in this body, I bear the simple truth that the Spirit of God renews belief in creation within each person and generation.

New creation, however, is not dependent on strength, or even on my own strained efforts to bring it into being. Instead, grace comes to meet me in the paradox of my illness. I am learning what Sylvia knew all along: the outwardly barren place is fertile precisely because of its vulnerability.

In moments of struggle, Sylvia comes to me with her faith that someday her children will understand the ongoing presence of God. I touch that holy expectancy in my own doubts, and I am no longer afraid. To overcome fear is to live in the City of God, a place where the angel's promise of fidelity echoes in the tender womb of our lives. Deeply rooted, I then know the daring of Mary's response: "Let it happen to me as you have said." And in the virgin, desert soil, hope blooms in anticipation of God's own birth.

THE VISITATION

*"Yes, blessed is she who believed
that the promise made her by God would be fulfilled."
(Luke 1:45)*

The rain had been relentless. There had been no break in the weather for several days and spirits were as soggy as the mud underfoot.

On this dreary July day, sheets of rain battered the window as I stood before a gathering of women. I'd been forewarned that this was not a talkative group, especially when it came to spiritual matters. I'd been told not to be disappointed if the group had nothing to say, if my attempts to lead them in reflection failed.

And so we started the reflection with a reading and a prayer. I had chosen the reading from Luke's gospel that tells the joyful story of Mary's visit to Elizabeth. Liturgically and emotionally, the reading seemed quite out of season. The summer rain pounded on the windows as we listened to the tale of Mary's journey.

Mary, filled with the joy of the annunciation, wasted no time in visiting Elizabeth. We can assume that she traveled far to share with a woman of her own flesh and blood. Mary and Elizabeth had something compelling to say to each other—both women were moved by the unexpected life within them. Their meeting was a joyous one in which both expressed wonder, awe, and surprise. Quite simply, in their greeting, God spoke to God.

As we read the gospel that summer day, I silently prayed that the conversations these women would have with each other might be touched with some of the same qualities.

After a brief prayer, I formed small groups and asked the women to reflect together on the meeting between Mary and Elizabeth. I suggested that they frame their reflections within Elizabeth's description of the baby leaping within her womb. I asked them to reflect on the reality of God leaping within them in their own lives. I posed this question to the groups: "What was the original spark of life—the leaping of God within you—that led you to make a significant decision in your faith life?"

At first, there was silence in the room. Then gradually the women began to speak softly to each other. As the energy in the room picked up, there was a shift to lively, animated discussions. The conversations became so spirited that the groups were disappointed when I announced that we needed to come back together as a large group. While shifting and dragging their chairs back into place, the women continued to talk with each other.

I asked the groups to report on their experience with each other. The room again fell silent. Just as I was starting to get nervous, an older woman stood up, wearing her life experience like a precious jewel. She looked me straight in the eye and said, "My dear, we decided that you asked the wrong question. What originally brought us to our life choices is interesting enough, but we didn't talk about that for very long. It is in the past. The really interesting story is what led us to remain faithful to those choices."

The nods around the room told me that the wisdom of the group had prevailed against my wrong question. It was not the initial leaping of life that they wanted to talk about; they wanted to bear witness to what had happened since. The women I had foolishly feared would be silent carried stories of new life that were a proclamation of Christ.

There had been much suffering in the group. Most of the women had lost their husbands, some had carried for years the agony of burying children. They had lived through wars and occupations both as victors and as refugees.

The stories these women told repeated a common theme. The care of other people, the meeting of faith with faith had returned the spark of life that "made them stay" faithful, even in the most desperate circumstances. What had held them firm in their faith and life commitments was the community of people who had supported them, taught them ways of overcoming adversity, and loved them through life's changes and crises. They had come to understand that new life is often born in the most unexpected circumstances. As a result, they expected that at any time they could meet kin along the road and feel the presence of God leap within them.

The women whom no one had expected would talk proclaimed the Magnificat in their stories. They recognized the presence of God in each other. These women had spoken truths so eloquently that their stories and longings deeply touched my own heart. New life leapt within me as I listened. We captured a moment of visitation. I learned that afternoon to keep my ego and doubts out of the way so that individual stories of faith could leap forward and be told, could become a meeting place of the Spirit.

That stirring of life is beautifully depicted in a wood carving at the Cloisters Museum in New York City. Mary and Elizabeth stand facing each other, their hands placed gently on each other's swollen wombs. They appear to be silent in this greeting, joined in the common experience of bearing new life with all of its mystery and uncertainty. Yet clearly they recognize divine life in each other—and Elizabeth's unborn child is joyful. The visitation is a vivid expression of Christian spirituality—the divine presence within me leaps in response to the presence of God in another. By recognizing the presence of God in each other, our hearts are reborn.

Mary's visit to Elizabeth illustrates these fundamental truths of the spiritual journey. Mary sets out on a long journey to visit Elizabeth, to share the mystery of their pregnancies, to marvel at God's wondrous deeds. Both unborn children are gifts of God. Elizabeth, thought to be barren, carries a child who leapt in response to the voice of Jesus' mother. That Elizabeth's child will declare the way for Jesus is foreshadowed in that leap. The gift of God within Elizabeth recognizes God's child. Feeling that recognition, Elizabeth proclaims Mary blessed.

The language of the Magnificat bridges the gap between our experience of sin in the world and the proclamation of God's presence. The Magnificat is a song of liberation that places the individual experience of God's fidelity directly in the context of the history of Israel. When Mary speaks, she gives praise to the God who has looked upon her lowliness—her humiliation at the pregnancy (in some sources, her status as a tainted, abused woman)—and exalted her.

These concrete words and actions—"filled the starving with good things," "pulled down princes from their thrones"—represent a tactile expression of God's presence. The reversal in the story, the confusion of the proud of heart, foreshadows the whole of the gospel and particularly the resurrection. The order as we have known it, the forces that would oppress Mary, the concrete suffering of the hungry and the poor are all addressed with force in the Magnificat. Mary speaks as a prophet of the poor with clarity and with force. When he hears these words of promise and reversal, the infant leaps in recognition; the conversion begins anew.

Our own conversion deepens as we begin to understand the ways in which God is active in our lives. We are called to spiritual growth through each other. Reflecting on the visitation and praying the Magnificat create space in our spirituality for speaking the truth of experience—particularly when that truth needs to be addressed with clarity and with force.

Spirituality that speaks one heart to another is nourished by the promise that God will let us know when we are asking barren questions; no new life will be experienced. The call to be with the poor, to accompany people "to the border" in their own reality, to alleviate burdens, to be hopeful, and to recognize God's lifting up of the abused and humiliated means that our individual spirituality is constantly interacting with the "bigger picture."

Our lives, our hearts, and the reality of the world make it quite evident that the forces of silencing and abuse, the gap between the hungry and the rich, the poor and the powerful enjoying the view from the throne are as near to us as summer rain. So too is the calling to create a space where God can leap within us, and dwell there for a long, long time.

THE NATIVITY

"Look! The virgin is with child and will give birth to a son
whom they will call Emmanuel,
a name which means 'God-is-with-us.'"
(Matthew 1:23)

The subway platform was noisy, crowded, dark, and cold. While I waited for the train, I noticed posters warning that rat poison had recently been spread about the station. The public address system crackled with an announcement informing passengers that there would be a delay because of police activity farther down the subway line. The announcement continued with an advisory that passengers stand away from the edge of the platform and exercise caution while entering and exiting the trains. Someone had recently been pushed from the platform by a mentally ill man and awareness of danger was higher than usual.

The warnings of danger, anxieties about delayed trains, and the depressing atmosphere of the station seemed worlds away from the bright Christmas decorations on the streets.

My time on the platform contemplating rat poison and a lost Christmas spirit paid off in the end. I was near the front of the crowd when the train pulled into the station and, as a result, was able to get a seat. Because this was not going to be a quick trip, I was grateful to be sitting. I needed to ride from one end of Manhattan to the other and the police activity had forced me to take the local line.

One stop at a time, the shifts in the crowd reflected the diversity of New York City and, in microcosm, the world. The briefcases of Wall Street yielded to mothers and children, medical personnel, office workers dressed for holiday luncheons, custodians, and people whose clothes were ragged. The language changed from English to Spanish, Chinese to Italian to sounds I did not recognize. Mostly, however, people were silent.

For all of its noise, color, and motion, the subway is often ridden in solitude. It is possible in this underground space to watch the world go by and yet to be quiet with one's thoughts and one's God.

The degree to which that connection to God is possible became apparent to me that dreary December day. Too restless to read, I closed my book and looked around the subway car. I saw that the woman across the aisle from me was reading her well-worn bible. A gentleman at the end of the car was fingering black beads that looked like my Grandpa Kennedy's rosary—except that what the man reverently held were Muslim prayer beads. The Jewish man next to me wore a yarmulke and prayer shawl, ever aware of the presence of God. Across the aisle sat a little girl wearing a medal of our Lady of Guadalupe.

It struck me that I was traveling in sacred space, no less so because we were all passing through underground tunnels where rodents and darkness reign. I often pray on the subway, sometimes with complex laments such as "Now what?" but also at times with a sense of comfort and wonder. I was deeply moved to discover that the same is true of other people.

That day I became more alert to the subway prayers. For the length of Manhattan, one stop at a time, I witnessed people reading their holy books, standing silently, or holding something of significance to their faith. The longing for God is deeply present on the local train and, in those longings, Christ is born.

Much to the consternation of the mayor of New York, homeless people live in the subway tunnels. They beg and they also say their prayers on the trains. There are signs in the cars reminding passengers that it is against the law to beg in this way. In the face of such warnings and the fears they provoke, it requires a certain courage to listen to the stories of the dispossessed, even when they wear "charity credentials" around their necks like holy medals .

On the day I noticed the subway prayers, a duly authorized man entered the car and began to speak:

Brothers and sisters, do not be afraid of me. I will not hurt you. I am homeless and hungry but I am like you. I once rode the trains to work but then I lost my job and my apartment. I was desperate until I met with kindness from the St. Agnes Food Bank. I now carry food to feed those who are hungry. If there is anyone here who needs something to eat, I have food in my bag. If anyone here would like to make a donation, I am registered to receive funds. Even a penny matters.

The man worked his way through the car, offering sandwiches to the hungry. With his other hand, he accepted donations coaxed out of lint-filled pockets and soft, leather briefcases. In the presence of the silent longings for God, the man used the term "brothers and sisters" not as a threat, but as a call to solidarity with the homeless ones of Bethlehem.

I must admit that I like my manger scenes neat and tidy, without the animals, the blood, and the contradictions. But that day I could not miss the fact that a subway car and the people within it bore witness to the birth of Jesus. The name "Emmanuel" means that the nativity happens not in the prettiest of places, but in the midst of the struggles and joys of human life. The prophet Isaiah declared that the baby named Emmanuel would create a home for the people of Israel. "God with us" restores wholeness in the midst of brokenness and exile.

Isaiah also said that no one can know the mind of God, or predict the places where God will be revealed. Surely this is most tenderly shown by the "King of kings" who comes to earth as a vulnerable, dispossessed infant. The child who will reveal a new home with God lies in a borrowed manger. Later he will be carried by his mother into Egypt, a refugee in the place where the ancestors of the House of David lived as slaves. Later still he will call to us in our own day and time to open the doors of our hearts and welcome the paradox of his birth.

We find the baby's manger not in the castles, but in the subways and stables of our lives. The certain, the arrogant, the rich, and the proud within and around us will not want this to be true. We will not necessarily like this vulnerable mother and child. Yet Jesus is born in the places of contradiction and weariness: the hope that has worn thin, the heart that has suffered, the burned-down houses, and prayer uttered in underground spaces. Jesus is born in the joy of the familiar and in the terror of uncertainty. Jesus is born on the local train, God with us in the flesh and bone of our longings and our hungers. And before this manger scene, my heart falls silent in awe to pray.

THE PRESENTATION
IN THE TEMPLE

"Now, Oh God, you are letting your servant go in peace
as you promised;
for my eyes have seen the salvation
which you have made ready in the sight of the nations."
(Luke 2:29-31)

Hulda lived in a small house near the bend in the road that is Kendallville, Iowa. The last town before the Minnesota border, Kendallville is a small collection of houses, a gas station, and a bar and grill tucked into the rolling hills and invisible from a distance. Just north of the town proper runs the Upper Iowa River, a narrow but rapidly moving Mississippi tributary that attracts strangers with canoes and local residents carrying fishing poles.

The Upper Iowa was Hulda's favorite fishing river for most of her ninety-four years. She fished in private places, the locations of which were known only by

Louise, her half-sister, fishing partner, and best friend. Passing canoes and automobile passengers never spotted Hulda and Louise. Even in their advanced years, both women knew how to climb a fence and hide in the brush where people and fish would never detect their presence.

The hardest part of this invisibility was hiding Hulda's ladder. Hulda had been unable to climb over fences unassisted since the 1960s when she had broken her femur. For some reason, the bone had never quite healed. As a result, Hulda was in constant pain for the last twenty-five years of her life.

Hulda consulted a number of doctors about the pain. She even made a pilgrimage to the Mayo Clinic where she discussed surgical options and medical risks with orthopedic specialists. Ultimately she was advised to accept the fact that there was little that could be done to correct her leg; pain would simply be part of her life. Hulda heard the news, accepted it, and decided to keep fishing—albeit with a ladder in tow. For Hulda, pain was no reason to stop living.

It was a lesson that Hulda knew well; the pain in her femur was hardly her introduction to adversity. Hulda had been a farm wife during some of the century's most difficult years for agriculture. She had lived through the swirling, dusty droughts of the Great Depression. To coax life from the land was a struggle that Hulda had undertaken with courage and perseverance. It was the same kind of courage and perseverance that

Hulda had applied to the human relationships in her life, relationships that could be as unforgiving as the dustbowl climate. Life was filled with struggle, yet Hulda's spirit was as legendary as the starkness of the depression years. Her eyes sparkled with the presence of vitality and humor. Hulda's farmhouse and later her home in Kendallville were hospitable places. Hulda kept baked goods stacked in her freezer in case a guest should arrive. No one ever left her home or her presence lacking for any kind of nourishment.

Hulda had about her a spirit of compassion and warmth that deepened with each new round of her own pain. She wrote a column for the local newspaper, a piece that, in the hands of a lesser person, could have become a "gossip column." Instead, Hulda wrote her stories of life in Kendallville as a narrative of human connections. Her writing was respectful and accurate, her mind inquisitive and active. She missed nothing.

Hulda would not have called herself a holy woman, but she was. Hulda allowed struggle and pain to transform her into the most open of souls. She did not judge; she did not exclude others. Anyone could talk to Hulda, and everyone did so without fear of betrayal. Hulda's radiance and hospitality led people to her. She worshiped regularly at the local Lutheran church. Hulda knew the hymns and prayers by heart where she carried them alongside her struggles, her joys and her memories. Because of her long faith journey, Hulda recognized holiness when she saw it in others. When Hulda recognized goodness, love, and faith in another person, she called the presence by its proper name: God.

Hulda was destined by her very long life to bear the pain of losing those she had loved through time. Louise was buried during an ice storm that came early in the season, froze the branches, and made the surface of the cemetery so slippery and dangerous that Hulda could not walk to the grave. She was deeply sad that day, but held firm in her faith that Louise was in God's care and that she would be "seeing her again soon."

Hulda cared about and was receptive to the pain of others, offering sympathy to those who sought to comfort her. That summer Hulda fished in plain sight, her partner and her ladder no longer physically present but alive in her memory.

Hulda dared to believe in God's promise without knowing when her own suffering would end. She was a great witness to the presence of God in life. In pain until the last of her days, Hulda never stopped recognizing and seeing Christ present in the sanctuary of her life and her world. The night she died, my husband dreamed about Hulda standing tall on strong legs. Her faith had made her whole, she had now seen God face to face.

Broken and whole, images of Hulda remain with me. They beckon like the prophecies spoken by Simeon and Anna when Jesus was presented at the temple. These prophets, devout in a faith that had been nourished and nurtured over a lifetime, recognized in Jesus the fulfillment of God's promise to Israel. Simeon predicted to Mary that Jesus would suffer. He warned Mary that her own heart would be broken and he praised the generosity of God. Simeon was faithful enough to know that the generosity and suffering were somehow linked in God's revelation.

Anna, too, had the purity of heart to know God's son when she saw him. In her old age, she praised God and spoke of Jesus to all who would listen. Anna's faith—like Hulda's—had grown through time and loss. The promise of deliverance was concrete in her experience, brokenness and wholeness together present in the infant lovingly carried into the temple.

Hulda recognized the presentation of Jesus in the sanctuary of her own life. She bore witness to that presence in her love and care for others. As Simeon prophesied to Mary about Jesus, Hulda's pain over the years laid her heart bare. The truth that emerged is that love is concrete, faith is a gift in the most difficult of times, and often—very often—both the prophets and the infant Jesus are present in our midst.

By some standards, Hulda's life was unremarkable. Yet, by the faith and love she inspired, Hulda was a prophet living at the temple gate. It was not a preponderance of words that made the generosity of God so apparent in her spirit. Hulda's gift was a faith that kept her sitting by the Upper Iowa River, like the prophetess Anna at the temple, ready to greet salvation when she saw it.

Having met God in human form, Hulda experienced the presentation in the temple as a daily event. And when the stranger was presented at her door, without hesitation, Hulda invited God in for coffee and cake. Her life and her hospitality were Hulda's continual song of praise.

FINDING THE CHILD
IN THE TEMPLE

"Why were you looking for me?
Did you not know that I must be in my Father's house?"
(Luke 2:47, 51)

Late one October afternoon, I decided to be adventuresome in the kitchen. As usual, I found myself cooking too fast and under time constraints. When I discovered that I was missing a key ingredient for my pasta dish, I prevailed upon my son Patrick to walk a half a block to the corner store. He was eight years old, so running an errand for Mom was still a special thing. He shot out the door, money in his pocket, with a promise to be right back with the ingredient and the change.

Patrick did not come right back. After twenty minutes had gone by, I decided to go search for him. Then, just as I was getting ready to leave, Patrick came in the front door with an impish grin on his face. In one hand

he held the bag from the store; the other hand was behind his back.

"I'm sorry that I took so long," he said as he handed me the grocery bag, "and I'm sorry that I spent all of the change. But I got you these." With pride and love, he handed me a bouquet of flowers from the neighborhood florist. The flowers were three pink roses.

When I hugged him, Patrick said, "The flower lady told me there were some flowers that I could have for you, but they were old. I said that I wanted to give you fresh flowers, so she sold me these." (At a major discount, I thought.)

Patrick got a vase down from the cupboard and together we put the roses on the piano. "I thought that you would like these because you like roses," he said. And with that statement, he went outside to play.

I presume that Patrick did not know all that is involved in my love of roses. The symbolism of the rose stretches far beyond my personal preferences. The rose is an ancient symbol of unity, harmony, paradox, and life from death. In Christian spirituality, the rose symbolizes the death and resurrection of Christ, the purity of Mary, and love—both human and divine.

The rose, with all its historical symbolism, has become for me a personal reminder that there is beauty among the thorns, an explosion of life in the face of death and, in the dead of winter, a promise of spring. The power of the rose is such that it has become a centering point for me in some of the most difficult moments of my life. I've taken to planting roses when life deals its disappointments. I've planted many rosebushes, digging out a place where fears, anxieties, and sorrows are rooted and transformed. The rosebushes are gentle reminders of the renewal of life. They symbolize peace.

Whether or not Patrick knew all of this, he chose to express his love by buying me roses. It was a beautiful, spontaneous gesture by my child. Somehow it came as no surprise to realize later in the evening that the roses had arrived on the feast of Thérèse of Lisieux. Her promise to shower the world with roses as a sign of God's love had been fulfilled for me that day through my son.

Most days present far too few opportunities to celebrate who we really are. I am inclined to believe that the bits of knowledge, the fragments of self that I meet in the course of the day are the whole truth. It is only infrequently that I stop and appreciate the presence of God in the whole of my life, in the center of my world. My search for God can be as rushed and impatient as my marginal cooking. Frantically looking for God can lead me to emptiness. The gift of the roses was a reminder to look for God in love miraculously present within the demands of the moment.

The story of finding Jesus in the temple makes a great deal more sense to me since Patrick unexpectedly brought me flowers. When he did not return as expected, I headed toward the door feeling the instinctive terror of a parent looking for a child.

Mary and Joseph must have felt that kind of panic when they discovered Jesus missing. They went searching for him among friends and relatives, first looking in the obvious places. Their search took them back to Jerusalem in the hope that retracing their steps would reveal Jesus. Their panic, their journey, and their searching mirror the experience of any parent who has looked for a child, and of anyone who has deeply longed for God. The three days of searching for Jesus foreshadow the days in the tomb—the in-between space of the paschal mystery wherein resurrection and beauty are as much a matter of faith as roses growing from harsh branches.

One of the interesting parts of the story is that, when Mary and Joseph finally find Jesus in the temple, he is surprised that his parents were looking for him. Jesus never considered himself lost. He was safe, comfortable, and engaged in conversation that astounded the teachers in the temple. Jesus' words to his exhausted parents—"Why were you looking for me? Did you not know that I must be in my Father's house?"—seem to go straight to Mary's heart. At that moment of reunion, the deepest truth emerges. Mary, through the darkness of her womb and the fidelity of her nurturing, has brought forth the Light of the World. And she has found Jesus again in the heart of the temple, the place where she should have expected him to be. She recognizes the gift Jesus brings and treasures it in her heart.

I pressed the roses Patrick gave me and put them in the drawer where I keep precious things. The memory of Patrick's temporary absence and the holiness of his gift are signs to me of finding Jesus in the temple of my own heart, in the chaos of my evening kitchen. The life journey, stretched and pulled as it is, finds its center in welcoming grace as a gift.

Jesus is never really lost in the fragments of life; to find him, I must simply embrace the mystery of the roses. All of life is holy. All of the fragments of searching for God are united in the moment of recognition and reunion. We find Jesus in the temple of our day-to-day hearts.

The Mysteries of Light

THE BAPTISM
IN THE JORDAN

"I baptize you with water for repentance,
but one who is more powerful than I is coming after me....
He will baptize you with the Holy Spirit and fire."
(Matthew 3:11)

The first sentence of Genesis describes the holy wind hovering over the waters of the earth. The primary acts of creation are the separation of the water from the sky, the dry land from the sea, the cycles of day and night. Water is the sustaining element of life; only oxygen is more important for human beings to survive. All living things are born of water and sustained by staying near to this life source. We die from dehydration much more quickly than from starvation. Human life depends on the water that runs through our veins; the salt content of our body and blood, our sweat and our tears mirrors that of the sea. Water drawn today from the Dakota aquifer is rain that fell when Jesus walked in Galilee.

There is no time in the history of creation that is not held in the deep blue waters of the earth.

The waters of the earth are interconnected and eventually become one. This relational quality of water was demonstrated in a humorous way when a storm in the South China Sea caused a ship to lose a container filled with thousands of small rubber ducks manufactured as bathtub toys. The little ducks have traveled the seas for years and washed up on every continent. A storm in a faraway sea tosses its captives on familiar shores, leaving us to wonder at the oneness of a planet so often thought of in divisive constructs. The waters of earth contain our sins as well as our salvation; the life source contaminated on one side of the earth will find its way into the bloodstream of another continent.

One of the most pressing issues of our time and human history is a lack of clean water. Diseases, birth defects, and preventable deaths often have their source in unclean wells. There are significant droughts caused by changing weather patterns induced by global warming. Our current thirst for living water carries an echo of ancient times. The prophet Isaiah invites the weary people of Israel to

Come to the water, all you who are thirsty;
though you have no money, come.
Pay attention, come to me;
listen and you will live. (Isaiah 55: 1, 3)

Isaiah uses the imagery of water to comfort those who have been worn down by exile, poverty, and innumerable losses. The love of God to be revealed by Christ will be an everlasting spring to those who listen. It is no surprise that each of the gospels introduces the ministry of Jesus with the story of John the Baptist. Jesus' cousin came from the barren desert hills of Judea to practice a baptism of repentance and forgiveness for sin. The baptism offered by John in the waters of the River Jordan was both a purification of the body by the water and a call to cleanse the soul through upright conduct. John's baptism is an inclusive invitation; all of good heart and the desire for repentance are called to and accepted for baptism regardless of their place of origin. John opens the baptismal waters to all people; the baptismal waters come from the same source and bless all who are touched by them. As he is baptizing, John announces that there is one who will follow him, one much greater than himself. His is the voice in the wilderness announcing that the reign of God is at hand. John in his open invitation to new life proclaims the presence of Christ on earth.

When Jesus comes to the Jordan, he must persuade John to baptize him. John considers himself unworthy to so much as untie Jesus' sandals, let alone offer him baptism. John is but the first person of many who will encounter Jesus and consider themselves unworthy to be in his presence, let alone play a part in salvation history. Jesus tells John that their relationship is just as it should be at that moment; John is not the Christ, but he is the one called to announce that the good news has arrived. John surrenders to this mystery and agrees to baptize Jesus. Together they stand in the sacred river and so begins a new creation. The baptism of Jesus is a public event that, like every baptism, is a gift both to and from the community. Those who witness Jesus' baptism know that something extraordinary is happening, even as they may lack the ability to describe it. The baptism initiates Jesus' public ministry and lets the waters of life flow among the people of God. The theme of living water will be present in much of Jesus' life and in his tender encounters with those he meets.

The gospel tells us that after all the people had been baptized and Jesus had received his own baptism, he withdrew to pray. This is a pattern that Jesus will follow throughout his public ministry. After great manifestations of grace, Jesus withdraws to pray to the One who sent him. The prayer of Jesus always leads him back into public ministry, regardless of whether or not the engagement with the world is pleasant for him at a particular moment. Jesus' prayer and his relationship with humanity always flow into each other. Each moment of presence affects the other. While Jesus was at prayer after his baptism, the heavens opened up in a tangible, physical way. The Holy Spirit descended on him in the form of a dove.

Noah sent out doves to explore the earth after the destruction of the great flood. The first doves did not return, indicating that the waters and the earth had not yet separated. When the second dove returned with an olive branch in its mouth, creation had been restored. The dove is a sign of life and peace; the offering of the olive branch is a symbol for imaging renewed possibilities. It is not incidental that the Holy Spirit appears in the form of a dove following Jesus' baptism. The word revealed by the dove is that Jesus is the beloved of God. We, like the people of Israel, are called to come to this living water, listen, pay attention, and be born again. The dove will come again at the time of Pentecost and in the quiet moments of our lives when we realize that Jesus Christ does indeed make all things new. Our baptismal invitation is to listen to the voice of the one who loves us through Christ; it is a tender calling and one that we hear with a sense of awe.

Like John the Baptist, we are called into the mystery in which we have a part to play by announcing that through Jesus, God is with us in a way unimaginable until we meet him in the waters of baptism. Since many of us were baptized as infants, it is often in standing witness to the baptism of our own children or new members of the faith community that we come to an appreciation of the power of these baptismal waters. When we agree to live as people who have been changed by the flowing of Christ into our lives, we promise to nurture the faith of those entrusted to our care. Each of us came into being in the presence of the faith community. We often feel unworthy or incapable of such witness. Who are we to touch the sandals of God? Yet we are called to the water with a spirit of grace and healing. When we imagine new possibilities, respond to the needs of others, or offer gratitude we are announcing the presence of Christ. To listen and to pay attention to the presence of God among us is to step again into the sacred Jordan and embrace its mysteries. There we know that we stand with Jesus as the beloved of God.

THE WEDDING FEAST AT CANA

"Everyone serves the good wine first, and then
the inferior wine after the guests have become drunk.
But you have kept the good wine until now."
(John 2:10)

It was an unexpected joy to be invited to the wedding of a man I had known since his birth. We had been childhood neighbors. I am just enough older than he to remember him when he was an infant, a toddler, a young man. The wedding was held in New York City, but many of the guests were people from Iowa whom I had known as a child. We gathered at the reception and began the exchange of stories that is possible between people with a common past. We spoke in the code of shared experience. The mention of a particular person or place from the neighborhood evoked the recollections and laughter of everyone gathered in our group. I discovered that things long forgotten become clear again in storytelling. We did not all remember the same things with clarity and the challenge of a different perspective

on a story was offered more than once. Between us we were able to piece stories together in a way that made them comprehensible to people who had grown up on other blocks and in other towns.

We recalled magical moments, such as ice skating in the street after a winter storm, the shared losses of grandparents, parents, and classmates. The borders and outlines of individual memories were stretched and filled in with details immediately recognized as true. The storytelling led to a profound sense of belonging. We have known each other from the beginning of our lives, an association that grows more meaningful as we age. Dancing in the ballroom of a fancy midtown hotel, we commented that we were a long way from the playgrounds where the dramas of our childhood had played out. We could not have known then about the turns our lives would take, the ground we would cover, or how we would one day bless the memories of our original place. In the space of that evening, we looked back and knew more about the ground in which we had been planted. The stories we told held a shared truth about our lives that led to a deeper understanding of who we had become. The bride learned more about the childhood of her new husband as she was welcomed into the circle of strangers' stories. It was an evening of great joy.

Weddings naturally lead to the telling of stories. One family learns the rooting stories of another as the bride and groom join to create something new. People from different places gather with unique histories that blend in the celebration to become a new, shared story. We eat and dance at weddings because the coming together breaks open the mysteries and gifts of life that we have come to treasure over time and hope to recognize anew in the day-to-day reality of our relationships. Weddings are joyful moments of transition that join the individual life story with the larger human story of love, hope, and generativity. We celebrate in the wedding feast our universal connection to God and to each other.

Weddings in the time of Jesus were celebrations that lasted for several days. There was rich hospitality that recognized the difficult journey made by the guests. As in our own time, there was a desire on the part of the host to care for the guests through an abundance of food and drink. There was dancing and praying, storytelling, the meeting of new people, and the creation of an enlarged sense of family. The weddings were days of jubilee. We do not know who was married in Cana a few days after Jesus was baptized and called his first disciples. We know from the gospel of John that it was in the context of a wedding that Jesus revealed the miracle of God's graciousness. Because Jesus and Mary were both there, one person in the couple was likely a family member. We see in the presence of Jesus and Mary at the wedding a depth of engagement in human life. It is not a great stretch of the imagination to see Jesus dancing and feasting at the wedding, since he would later use those images in his preaching.

After the party has been going on for some time, it becomes known that there is no more wine for the guests. To come up short in this regard would be a source of humiliation for both the host and the guests. Concerned when she learns that there is no more wine, Mary turns to Jesus for assistance. Jesus responds by saying that his hour of glory has not yet come. He refers not to the glory of the signs and miracles that will follow in the gospel narrative but to his death and resurrection. When he answers Mary's call to assist at the wedding, Jesus has already begun the transition into his public life and ministry. The true glory of God will be revealed slowly in the words, deeds, and person of Jesus. Mary's suggestion that the servants should do whatever Jesus tells them is recognition that something new is being created, even though its full meaning will not be immediately known. That something new will come into fullness only through the passion and resurrection of Jesus. But at this moment of beginning, Jesus is called to an act of compassion that tells us much about his life on earth. Jesus responds to the needs of those invited to the wedding banquet. No one shall want for anything at this celebration; deliverance from the potential shame of empty crocks will reveal something new about God's relationship with history.

Jesus tells the servants to gather six of the stone jars that are used for the prescribed cleansing and purification rituals of each day. The jars are large and hold between fifteen and twenty gallons of water. As the servants fill and carry the jars, they must be wondering what Jesus intends to do with ordinary water meant for ritual purification. We do not see or hear about Jesus making dramatic gestures or pronouncements. The water of the ordinary is quietly transformed into the wine of celebration. Those present at the wedding are unaware that anything unusual has happened. The presence of Jesus is enough for this powerful change to occur. It is with utter amazement that the steward discovers that the new wine is of the finest quality—made available at a point in the celebration when the host could likely get by with a less splendid wine. What is given instead is a generous, abundant flow of the finest wine just at the point when less is expected.

We sometimes grow weary in the rejected places of our lives, with the worn thin jars, the bits and pieces of unclaimed stories, and the unexpected moments of decision when the choices we make tell us who we are. We would sometimes like to send away the people who come to us for hospitality. Yet, when we are attentive, our own emptiness is often an invitation to conversion. God invites with a gentle whisper, not a mighty roar. Without loud sounds or fanfare, God slips the finest wine into our life stories in moments when experience has taught us to expect much less. It is then that we join our separate stories and find ourselves experiencing the abundant miracles that take place in God's household. Our stories are connected and changed like water into wine and we witness creation renewed.

PREACHING
THE KINGDOM OF GOD

"Let us go elsewhere, to the neighboring country towns,
so that I can proclaim the message there too,
because that is why I came."
(Mark 1:38)

The early European settlers in Wisconsin planted
mustard seed because they needed it for medicinal pur-
poses. Mustard seed can be used for a variety of conditions, including chest congestion, arthritis, and tooth-
ache. The medicinal uses of mustard seed were known
to the Chinese several thousand years ago. Mustard
seeds have also been found in the tombs of Egyptian
pharaohs, presumably because of the healing properties
of the herb.

Mustard grows wild all over the world. What the settlers in Wisconsin did not realize was that the type of
seed they planted is particularly tenacious. It can live in
the soil for seven years and regenerate as an uncontrolled

weed long after it is thought to have been eradicated. Mustard weed is expansive and will destroy anything in its path. There is a struggle today to save the native wildflowers of Wisconsin from mustard bushes that have been gaining strength for two hundred years. The lesson of the mustard seed is that those who deliberately plant it do so at their own peril.

The people who listened to Jesus knew that lesson well. It must have been terribly puzzling when Jesus offered the parable of the mustard seed. Jesus said that the reign of God is like a mustard seed that is sown in a field. The smallest of seeds becomes a large shrub where birds of the air find shelter.

Like all of Jesus' parables, the mustard seed story is short. Jesus never offers an explanation for the inconsistencies of the parables. As the Wisconsin settlers learned, planting mustard seed anywhere, let alone in a field where food is grown, is problematic. Why would anyone plant something that will lead to a struggle for containment? Those who first heard the parable knew the healing properties and the inherent dangers of mustard seed. Once it begins to grow, the plant changes the landscape in unpredictable ways. Shelter for the birds of the air? That image is incongruent with the reality of the growing season and the fact that, at the time of the year when birds need shelter, the mustard bush is not large enough to provide cover in its prickly branches. Scripture tells us that many people walked away from Jesus because they were unable to understand the meaning of parables. Some of them seemed to believe that Jesus was speaking in riddles to confuse instead of to enlighten.

It is through this kind of inconsistency, the turning upside down of familiar images and understandings, that Jesus proclaims the reign of God.

Jesus does not preach in a way that does violence to his listeners. Gently, through paradox, puzzles, and the breaking of barriers, Jesus invites us to enter the mystery of God's reign through the salt and yeast, seeds and weeds of ordinary life. Psalm 78 says:

> I will open my mouth in a parable;
> I will utter dark sayings from of old,
> Things that we have heard and known,
> That our ancestors have told us. (Psalm 78:2)

Jesus preaches a radical reversal of the power structures within society. Repeatedly he challenges us to look differently at the world, to question our assumptions about who God is and discover that the inauspicious beginnings of our faith might well become a shrub that can heal.

Jesus teaches through stories of relationship. The widow who approaches the judge for her just due is not simply giving us an example of persistence in prayer, though that may well be part of the message. She is also a profound example of a person on the absolute fringes of her society who dares to speak the truth to those who have power over her life. Her actions are as unheard of as deliberately planting mustard seeds. And what are we to make of the parable of the talents, a story about slaves entrusted by their master with sums of money that are outrageous; ten talents would have been several hundred years of wages. The image of a master entrusting his servants with his money speaks of crossing social divisions. It speaks of a generosity that borders on impossibility. It tells us not to fear our losses so much that we are incapable of living as stewards of a great treasure.

Matthew's gospel places the parable of the talents immediately before the description of the Last Judgment. The criterion for judgment is how we have treated each other, particularly those who are poor and in need. Our abundance of life is meant to be in service of others. Jesus preaches that we see God's face in the hungry and the poor. Those whom society rejects call upon us to invest ourselves in things that matter and, as St. Paul describes it, to alleviate the burdens of all. Jesus preaches again and again that we have been given the ability to recognize God in the puzzling and contrary moments in life. It is our choice whether we will see, hear, and respond.

Jesus' preaching makes clear that he knew the scriptures well. Luke's gospel describes Jesus going off to pray after his baptism. It is during this intense period of prayer that Jesus deals with the temptations to demonstrate his power in a self-serving way. In dealing with each temptation, Jesus comes to know his identity more deeply. He encounters the deep core that is God. When he returns to Nazareth, the belittled town of his childhood, he goes to the synagogue and finds in the scroll the words of the prophet Isaiah:

> The Spirit of the Lord is upon me,
> because he has anointed me to bring good news
>   to the poor.
> He has sent me to proclaim release to the
>   captives and recovery of sight to the blind,
> To let the oppressed go free,
> To proclaim the year of the Lord's favor.
>   (Luke 4:29)

When told that the scripture is being fulfilled in their midst, the people of Nazareth cannot think beyond their perceptions of Jesus as the son of Joseph, the kid they knew as he reached maturity, the one who has been living among them. It is inconceivable to them that the fulfillment of the scripture has been with them all along.

Their struggle is one that is familiar to us. Like those who listened to Jesus' preaching, we need new eyes to see the true reality of our lives. Jesus touched those who were cast aside in his culture: lepers, a woman with an unstoppable flow of blood, the dead bodies of Lazarus and Jarius' daughter. Jesus ate with sinners. He told a parable about a good Samaritan whose compassion was much greater than that of the people whose racism led them to view Samaritans as less than human. It is always tempting to read the gospel and wonder how those scribes and Pharisees could have been so blinded by their need to hold onto a familiar understanding of righteousness. We find it hard to believe that anyone in Jesus' presence could have failed to see that he was the Christ. Then comes the moment when we are faced with a homeless person who seems annoying, an oppressed person who seems frightening, when our best sense of humanity is overwhelmed by the suffering in the world. All of us know the desire to bury the talent for safekeeping, particularly when the understandings and perceptions that we hold dear are threatened.

Jesus preached a gospel that tells us to look beyond our immediate desires and perceptions so that we might discover the unexpected wonders of God. Jesus preaches in a way that confounds those who consider themselves wise. Those who are not so wedded to one understanding can see the hidden truths and recognize that preaching the word of God begins in universal love and returns there. Though that reality may seem as unthinkable as planting mustard seeds in the garden, it is the gospel of redemption, liberation, justice, peace, death, and resurrection that our hearts recognize as true.

THE TRANSFIGURATION

And he was transfigured before them,
and his face shone like the sun,
and his clothes became dazzling white.
(Matthew 17:2)

There are places on earth that call each generation of artists to look lovingly at their beauty. Often what makes these places special is the quality of light. The light changes and clarifies the wonder of the place. Artists are drawn to capture a moment of that light even as they know that what is revealed on the canvas is a transitory moment, a reality that can never be fully represented. The Hudson River Valley is such a place. Sometimes when I walk along the river there is such a piercing beauty in the light that I understand completely the longing to create a representative image of it. Every attempt I have made to do so has disappointed me. I have surrendered to the reality that I cannot capture that light in a photograph or drawing; the best I can do is sketch it and hold its power in my memory and imagination.

The particular beauty of one day's light cannot be preserved and carried in one's pocket. It is the essential quality of light to be ever changing; whatever the temptation to hold one vision dear, it must be surrendered for the light to retain its true nature. The purplish sky of December is by necessity quite different from the light of the summer solstice. No matter how compelling and beautiful the light is at a particular moment, it can be sustaining only if its rhythm is respected.

This human desire to preserve beauty and clarity was in evidence when Peter, James, and John went with Jesus to the mountaintop to pray. The presence of the disciples on the mountain bore witness to the love they experienced in Jesus and their desire to be with Jesus in prayer. Jesus had been preaching the reality that he would be killed at the hands of the elders, chief priests, and scribes. Peter in particular found the foretelling of the passion unacceptable. The disciples were likely relieved to be able to go to the mountain and escape having to think about the passion foretold by Jesus. They were alone on the mountain when the light shifted and the disciples found themselves witnesses to a new vision, a new way of seeing. They saw Jesus standing with Elijah on one side and Moses on the other. The presence of these two men, so important in the scripture and history of the Jews, indicated that Jesus was the fulfillment of both the law and the prophets. All that had been promised by God is fulfilled in Jesus. It is curious to realize that the disciples immediately recognized Elijah and Moses. Their stories were known, but their faces were not familiar. That the disciples recognized them speaks to their ability to see with the heart, to recognize the fulfillment of God's promise revealed in their midst. They were in that moment blessed with the gift of right vision—the ability to see God's face in the here and now.

The law represented by Moses provides the ethics for daily living. We are not to seek or worship false gods. For most of us, the graven images are not golden calves. Rather, we turn to technology, prejudice, or partial truths with the expectation that they will save us. That the truth of God is deeper than our own understanding and far surpasses the limits of human thought is sometimes too much to bear. So we break it down into smaller, more manageable pieces that we happily use to give orders to God. The most insidious of false gods is the belief that we know what is best for ourselves and for everyone else. To live in the presence of the true God is to listen more than we speak, to embrace mystery and be willing to be at a loss for understanding. We then incorporate the law for the purpose of loving, not as a cudgel or a weapon against others. The fulfillment of the law in Jesus tells us that the most important commandment is to love as we are loved.

The prophets called the people of Israel to fidelity during very troubled times in history. The people were

THE MYSTERIES OF LIGHT

reminded that God has always been faithful, and that fidelity is expressed in loving the poor and oppressed. Elijah was the greatest of the prophets; his call to fidelity foreshadowed and predicted the coming of Jesus. The fulfillment of the prophecy in Jesus means that God's fidelity has taken on our own flesh and blood. God is present in human history. God's beloved son, the one on whom God's favor rests, reveals a love that St. Paul will describe as higher and deeper than we can ask or imagine. That love breaks apart our categories and allows us to see the true movement of God in our lives.

The disciples watch in amazement as Jesus is surrounded by a light that makes his robes appear a dazzling white. "He was transfigured before them, and his face shone like the sun." (Matthew 17:2) They hear the echo of the words spoken at Jesus' baptism: Jesus is the beloved one of God, listen to him. Just as they have recognized Moses and Elijah, they come to an understanding of Jesus as Messiah and redeemer. This is the promised one whose fulfillment of the law and prophets leads to a new understanding of the reign of God. There is a *transfiguration*, a change in the person of Jesus that brings the light of the gospel into the world. As promised by the prophets, in this illumination the lowly are lifted up, the rich are sent away empty, the hungry are filled with good food, justice and peace kiss. The disciples experience absolute clarity about Jesus' identity and the faith they are called to live. Their awe at the events unfolding before them is palpable in the text. They are seekers who have found their lost home in God. Such moments of clarity and excitement always carry with them the temptation to preserve the experience and live in it forever without change or interruption. Peter immediately suggests that they construct three tents to preserve the presence of Elijah, Moses, and Jesus. He wants to live forever in the wonder of this moment, the beauty of this mountain where God so clearly dwells. Peter seeks to capture and preserve the wonderful light of this moment.

Peter is an endearing figure in part because he never hesitates to give orders to Jesus: let the passion not happen, let us build three tents, let the wonder of the moment not be shattered.

We are all blessed with days or experiences that we would seek to hold onto forever. The great moments in life such as the birth of a child, the joy of discovering something new, a particularly powerful experience of love are all awakenings that we want to preserve. Who wants to leave a quiet time by the ocean to go back to work? The very desire to hold onto clearly powerful moments in prayer or relationships can sometimes cause their clarity to disappear. We are meant to move and be moved by the process of light. As Jesus tells Peter, we cannot remain on the mountaintop where we have experienced something of great beauty. The disciples are told that they must go back to the joys and dangers of their

lives. Even more perplexing, they are told to hold sacred
the vision they have seen until the time comes for Jesus'
identity to be revealed in a larger way. They are not yet
allowed to tell their story. Perhaps this is because the extraordinary experience of the transfiguration must be
seasoned and translated by what happens when Jesus
turns his face toward Jerusalem. Peter, James, and John
do not understand the transfiguration as well as they
might think. Their knowledge will reach its fullness in
the death and resurrection of Jesus. Like the disciples,
we are witnesses to that light when we let go of our fear
and see the radiant, transfigured face of Christ in our
midst.

THE INSTITUTION
OF THE EUCHARIST

"I am the bread of life.
Whoever comes to me will never be hungry,
and whoever believes in me will never be thirsty."
(John 6:35)

The little boy played in the warm, aqua blue waters of the South Pacific Ocean. He splashed, ran to the beach and back into the water, laughed and exhibited a joyful spirit. I sat watching him with Sister Ceil, a Maryknoll sister and doctor. I commented to Ceil about the exuberance of the child and she told me his story. The boy had been brought at the age of two to the rehabilitation home founded by Sister Ceil. He weighed fourteen pounds. He was listless and near death. The first priority was to feed him. His condition made it necessary to gradually introduce the food to his system. As the weeks went by, he grew able to eat more solid food. After a month, his eyes began to lose their dullness.

The nutritious food seemed to awaken his body and spirit. He began to play. Within a year, the little boy was splashing before us in the ocean. "He will always be small for his age, but he is doing very well," said Sister Ceil. "It is amazing how quickly a child can come back to life when given good food."

The exuberance of a little one reborn after near starvation was a joy to see. I watched him play for several minutes, amazed by the tenacity of his spirit. Sister Ceil told me other stories about children who had become part of the community. Some of them had terrible handicaps and parents who lacked the resources to keep the children at home. Others suffered from birth defects or had sustained serious injuries. The rehabilitation center is almost a small town, with income-producing activities that also train the residents in a craft. Earlier in the day we had visited a bakery. Women and children sat around a large table, each with a circle of dough in front of them. They kneaded and twisted the dough into loaves of bread and small rolls. Some of the bread is eaten by the residents and much of it is sold to others.

While we sat watching the children playing in the water, rolls from the bakery were brought to us for a snack. Soon plates heaped high with rice also appeared, as did fruit and coffee. I was particularly aware of the food before me that day: a generous and hospitable offering that sated a hunger masked by the heat of the day. "Sometimes people don't realize they are hungry until they are in real trouble," noted Sister Ceil. "The best way to handle the heat is to eat one meal a day, all day long." We shared the Eucharist that day first in the chapel and again in the breaking of bakery bread brought into being by people whose lives were not easy. Eucharist translates as "thanksgiving." I was particularly grateful that day for the mystery of a journey that had led me to meet and break bread in an exquisitely beautiful place where children are coaxed back from the dead. Those of us who live in the presence of plenty do well to remember that our abundance is not shared by all.

Every culture on earth recognizes the importance of a common meal. Eating together is an experience of sharing the human need for nourishment and companionship. Whether a sandwich is being quickly shared or a ritual banquet is being served, the act of eating with others erases barriers. We all hunger for food that nourishes both the body and the soul. Particular foods are connected with individual and communal histories: families share the recipes for Grandma's rolls, societies remember historic events with dishes eaten only at a certain time of the year.

Jesus ate his last supper with his disciples during the season of Passover. The foods of Passover are offered in recollection of the passage from slavery to freedom. It is a feast of unleavened bread in remembrance of the fact that the swift passage out of Egypt did not allow time for the bread dough rise. God fed the people in the wilderness in the form of manna that had to be harvested and eaten quickly. It could not be stored or kept for another time. God gave the food needed in the moment and that food sustained life. The people were strengthened as they journeyed to the Promised Land. When Jesus broke the bread and offered it to his disciples, he did so within a very rich historical context and in anticipation of his own passion, death, and resurrection.

Jesus' gift of the Eucharist was given on the night of his betrayal. The Last Supper occurred on the brink of the disintegration of community and communion as the disciples had known these. Within hours, the disciples would scatter. Peter, eyewitness to Jesus' ministry and transfiguration, would claim that he did not know the man from Nazareth. I can understand his fear. The agony of the passion and the glorious mystery of the resurrection that would be revealed within the next few days began with a rupture of the world the disciples had come to know through their relationship with Jesus. Though Jesus had told his disciples that he would have to suffer and die, they had no way of imagining what that mystery would mean to them. They did not understand that Jesus' body would be broken and restored to life. They could not have known that they were about to be transformed in the passage from death to life. It is likely that the disciples wanted their relationship with Jesus to continue as it had been, for who would want to lose the presence of the one who revealed God's own truth?

When Jesus offered his disciples the bread and wine he transformed them by calling them his own body and blood. The offering of bread and wine is the final announcement of the new covenant revealed in Jesus Christ. Sins are forgiven, hope is restored, and all are welcome at the table. The food of God's own self that is given in Eucharist fulfills our deepest hungers. Our spirits are restored in the real presence of Christ within and around us. This communion gives us strength to make all of the waters of our lives baptismal. Fear, doubt, shame, or any other longing that might lead to internal or external violence instead becomes the entryway to conversion. The beloved of God is in our bodies and souls. When we accept the body and blood of Christ, we proclaim his resurrection in our own day and time. This shifts our perspective by making the love of God the very essence of our lives. It is amazing to see how quickly we can heal in God's presence, in the eating of good food that is nothing less than the source of all life; the bread of life kneaded, twisted, and transformed so that we might hold in our hearts the holy memory of God's fidelity. For Christ is with us always, yes, even to the end of time (Matthew 28:20). That real presence makes it possible for the most worn among us to be restored to the exuberance of a child at play in the waters of the earth.

The Sorrowful Mysteries

THE AGONY IN THE GARDEN

"Take this cup away from me.
But let it be as you, not I, would have it."
(Mark 14:37)

The pastor's voice broke as he told the story of the night the Guatemalan Army entered the village and destroyed it. Men, women, and children were massacred. Some died from bullet wounds, others died locked inside a church which the military men set on fire. All signs of life were threats to the State; all human works of faith and justice had to be destroyed.

Later, long after the screaming and the gunfire had receded into an agonizing silence, the priest risked his life by telling his story to the world. His eyes welled with tears at the paradox of such a beautiful, faithful people suffering so much horror. Their blood had been poured out on sacred ground because of a violence driven by blind greed and the lust for power. How terrible to know that somewhere, someone was so afraid of a faithful people that genocide in a garden was an acceptable option.

The violence was meant to inspire terror, and it did. At the same time, thousands of faithful people looked the monster in the eye, wished for a different outcome, and stood strong in spite of their fear. No one wanted to die, yet for many in vulnerable positions, a conscious decision was made to draw from the well of God's fidelity in the midst of the agony.

Guatemala is one of the most beautiful countries on earth, and yet unspeakable suffering took place there. Since the peace process has begun, the land has yielded testimony of horrible crimes and heroic courage. Dry bones are telling the story.

It is difficult and painful to imagine the breadth of the horror. Yet, the voices of those who suffered are being heard and, as impossible as it may seem, reconciliation is being imagined. Drinking again from the cup of suffering so that life may be restored is understood as being the will of God, the call and challenge of redemption. Truth is required to heal the wounds of the beautiful land.

The paradox of such agony in the garden is known to each of us. It is not distant experiences that cause us to question God or beg for a different outcome. The most profound experience of suffering, the most devastating knowledge of betrayal happens in the familiar places of life. It is within the deepest and most beautiful relationships, the areas of life about which we care the most, the intimate and treasured land, that truly agonized prayers are spoken. Trust is sometimes violated by those we love, relationships are severed by circumstances and by sin, at times decisions must be made that leave us torn apart, crying with what Matthew described as "sadness and anguish" (Matthew 26:37).

Life itself can betray us in the cherished spaces. The suffering of innocents in the world—from Guatemala to neonatal intensive care units—shakes up our treasured beliefs and understandings of the will of God. Who can understand or immediately accept the death of a child, mental illness, random and organized violence? Who, confronting such pain, would not beg God that the situation be changed? To come face-to-face with suffering that is inescapable and debilitating is to cry tears that turn to blood. How does one know the will of God when suffering strikes at one's own flesh and justice seems an empty promise?

It is not enough to simply declare that suffering is God's will, since to make that proclamation is, at times, to craft God as a cruel puppeteer. The complications increase when the reality and outcome of human sin is at work in our lives. There are too many aspects of life that we simply cannot explain away; reality demands that we pray our doubts and fears out loud.

Letting the dry bones tell their story brings us into the presence of the living God. In that intimate prayer, God leads us to deeper levels of understanding and the experience of unfailing love. It is then that we gain strength to go forward on paths that we might not choose, to be courageous in the midst of suffering we do not understand, to stand firm in the face of betrayal at the heart of life.

Mark's gospel describes the Mount of Olives— called "the garden" only in the gospel of John—as a place where Jesus went to rest, to be at home with God when his life and ministry had worn him out. This was a safe, familiar place where Jesus could look forward to being restored and renewed. It was a treasured place where he went with his friends. It was sacred ground.

There is no surprise in Jesus' going to the garden for comfort, for prayer, and for the gathering of strength. That he went to the Mount of Olives after the Last Supper seems only right. The intimacy begun with his friends at table continued in his encounter with God. Where else would Jesus go for rest but to this beautiful place that had, in the past, sustained his spirit?

Jesus was aware of the passion that lay ahead of him. The punishments of the Roman state had been devised to provoke fear. Jesus went to pray for a different outcome and to gather within himself the strength of God for the sorrow that was to come. He expressed his desire to avoid the suffering.

It was in a familiar, intimate place that violence and betrayal occurred; it was on sacred ground that the first blood of the passion flowed. And it was here that Jesus surrendered to a reality deeper than immediate events.

The surrender to God tempers Jesus' loneliness when his friends fall asleep. The deeper truth of God's fidelity gives Jesus peace when he is betrayed on the sacred ground of friendship.

Jesus' acceptance of God's will is an active choice. Jesus surrenders to the reality of redemption, but he does so in the midst of profound suffering and a struggle for life. The mystery of the passion itself is contained in his surrender. Letting go of one's own will and plans is letting go of power as the world defines it and living in the mysterious power of God. This type of acceptance is not arrived at easily, or without great struggle. Who among us wants to suffer the mysteries and fate of the one to be crucified?

Yet, back to the garden we must go. In the familiar, intimate places, we meet the realities of life that betray, threaten, and seek to destroy us. And in those sacred gardens, we find Jesus bearing witness to the truth. The garden blooms in a continued passage from death to life because it is rooted in God's transformation. Tears turned to blood and blood turned to faith reveal a will that runs deeper than sight.

God in the garden remembers all and gives us strength, even in the face of our most grievous mysteries. The call to surrender is an invitation to embody the conscious memory of God in the familiar suffering of our lives. Then and there, the passion begins anew.

THE SCOURGING

After having Jesus scourged,
he handed him over to be crucified.
(Matthew 27:26)

In my town there is a low brick building that serves as a recreation center. One corner of the building has been designated a "State of New York Cultural/Historic Center." The center, which features exhibits, is named "Up the River, Down the River" in honor of the two things for which Ossining is known. "Down the River" refers to the Croton Aqueduct, a nineteenth-century engineering marvel that brought potable water into New York City. "Up the River" refers to Sing Sing Prison.

Predictably, there is a great contrast between the two exhibits. One is filled with pride. The viewer can examine impressive engineering intricacies while listening to recordings of the soothing sound of water flowing through the aqueduct pipes.

The sound effects of the "Up the River" exhibit are tapes of prison noise. Artifacts of criminal punishment are exhibited, including a replica of a cell, the electric chair from Sing Sing, and detailed information about the practice of flogging prisoners.

During the nineteenth century, prisoners were flogged at Sing Sing both as punishment and as a means of intimidation. Prison narratives describe the cruelty of the process and the steps that were taken to make sure other prisoners heard the cries of agony. The instruments of torture were carefully made to inflict the greatest possible pain.

A model of the Sing Sing cat o' nine tails now hangs on the wall of the cultural center. School children marvel at the particulars of it. I also marvel, and I mourn that the violence and intimidation it represents are not static museum pieces. Beyond the fact that flogging is literally a contemporary reality, it is symbolic of what lies at the heart of human cruelty.

The practice of flogging—or scourging, as scripture describes it—is, unfortunately, as old as the establishment of social order. During prosperous times in ancient Egypt, slaves were plentiful and, as a result, could be flogged to death for minor infractions. A scourging death served notice that the lives of slaves were worthless. The scourging of slaves in the United States branded the results of racism, oppression, violence, and contempt into the scarred backs of a people torn from Africa.

Flogging—in ancient Rome, on the high seas, within the cold stone walls of nineteenth-century Sing Sing, or in contemporary Asian prisons—serves one key purpose: to maintain an established order through physical torture. It is also a means of dehumanizing the victim. The whips of the Egyptians, the Romans, U.S. slave holders, and prisons are remarkably similar. Human cleverness is put at the service of letting the victim know who is in control. Human dignity is destroyed along with the flesh.

The entire crucifixion process was designed to maintain order. Scourging was a common part of the Roman crucifixion process and was done in public places to terrorize onlookers. Destroying the dignity and flesh of the person being scourged was an expression of power. The scourging was also intended to speed up the subsequent death of the person on a cross. A person half dead as the result of scourging spent less time dying on the cross.

Some early biblical commentators believed that the desire to shorten the pain of the crucified person may have involved an element of mercy. However, it is difficult to reconcile mercy with scourging and crucifixion. I can't help but agree with later interpretations that a shorter period of time on the cross was simply more efficient for the Roman soldiers carrying out the execution.

Regardless of the multiple intentions and interpretations, the dehumanization of Jesus was intensified by the flogging. That is, perhaps, the essential meaning of brutally beating a human being. Whether inflicted upon a prisoner, a slave, or the Son of God, the staggering and potentially deadly pain of scourging degrades the victim by making him or her less than human. The one receiving the lash is not "human like us" but diminished by power, prejudice, and, in the case of Pontius Pilate, political expediency.

After Pilate had given in to the demands of the crowd, Jesus was subjected to the routine torture of the state. Just as Jesus had both a religious and a civil trial, so too his degradation had to occur on two levels. The treatment he received at the hands of those who tied him up and flogged him carried two messages: the religious authorities believed that he was not God and the state authorities, by their treatment of Jesus, cast doubt on whether he was to be considered human. The sentence of crucifixion was an indication that he was not thought to be worth the trouble he was causing. That Jesus was deemed dispensable was intended as a message to his followers—do not dare to cause the same kind of trouble.

This part of the passion narrative would be less disturbing if it were, like the Sing Sing whip, part of ugly past practices. We need only reflect on life experience and social realities to know that the opposite is true. Bitterness of heart easily divides the world into "we" and "they"—those whom we perceive to be human beings like ourselves and those who are different and, as a result, "less than." Those who are dehumanized are surely not children of God.

We spin together the scourging cords in various ways. Lack of attention to the health care needs of minorities and the poor weakens people; statistics bear out that they simply die more quickly, often from scourges and germs that are preventable or treatable. Tremendous violence is done in the name of religion. Differentiating who is a child of God from who is not makes it easier to condemn countries and next-door neighbors to death. Cultivation of any loathing for another human being carries within it the fanatical hatred that is so shocking when it erupts en masse. Religious wars have torn the world and its people apart. It requires only one account of a rape in Bosnia to know that violence against an individual is violence against all people, and violence against the love of God.

The scourging of Jesus was such an act of violence. In the efficiency of the executioner, the whole of the human capacity to tear the flesh and soul of troublemakers was visited upon the body of Jesus. We know that the scourging weakened him. We also know that there was perseverance on Jesus' part. Although gravely wounded, Jesus held within him a faith deeper than the reach of the lash. That gift of courageous faith is present in others who, when scourged and abused by power, retain within them the strength of the Spirit to resist the evil visited upon their flesh.

Mercifully and gratefully, the living God assures the dignity of every human being. Knowledge of that dignity unravels the whips and cords of everyday hatred that desperately weakens the body of Christ.

THE CROWNING WITH THORNS

And they stripped him and put a scarlet cloak round him,
and having twisted some thorns into a crown they put this on
his head and placed a reed in his right hand. To make fun of
him they knelt to him saying, "Hail, king of the Jews!"
(Matthew 27:28-29)

I have always secretly hoped that there is really only
one jeering crowd in history, a crowd that reappears in
times of turmoil, does its violence, and then slips away
for a while. The beauty of there being only one crowd
of people doing violence to each other is that "they"
would then be far away from me. I would neither fear
being victimized by those whose identity seems to de-
pend on hurting others, nor would I be tempted to join
a group that harasses people.

I would like my world to be safe from crowns of
thorns, from the destructive intent behind "Hail, King
of the Jews." I would like to believe myself incapable of
taunting the God who is among us. My hope is that I
would never need to plead forgiveness for lack of a hos-

pitable heart and mind. That hope is as much a fantasy as the phantom crowd unable to see the truth. The crowd and its taunts are within me, as close to the surface as the desire to put aside what can't be understood or tolerated.

I relearn this lesson whenever I find myself at home on a weekday. Our backyard abuts a school playground. It is remarkably quiet during the day except for the three times that the recess bell rings. At those times, the noise from the playground travels over the fence and I can hear the children playing. The joyful sounds are frequently interrupted by the sounds of children positioning themselves against each other. The jeering and the teasing take on familiar tones as I hear children say "You think you are so cool" and "If you're so smart, how come you can't figure out why no one likes you?"

There are teases that rhyme and a few crude charges and taunts yelled out as children wound each other. Mostly I am struck by the similarity of playground teasing today to the jeers and rhymes of my own childhood and, I suspect, to those of generations before me. Certainly the tone of voice remains the same, as does the need for one person or group to put down another.

It hurts a bit when I listen to the children over the fence because I know that, in fact, words can hurt you. I also know that jeering and teasing do not end with childhood and I realize that, in various ways, I have been part of the crowd on the playground. It is easy to dismiss people who I find hard to understand or whose values are different from my own. I can be as cruel as any school child when confronted with troublesome ideas or situations I cannot control.

There are moments when I believe that playground banter is in fact the model for discourse with anyone or anything that seems threatening in the world. From early childhood, patterns of words weave their way into our consciousness. And, contrary to our best hope, the language of making and taunting scapegoats tends to stay with us for life.

Historically, the scapegoat was seen as the creature that takes on the sin of the community and is either sacrificed or sent to wander in the wilderness. There are additional meanings. One is that, in human communities, the scapegoat is the person whose brilliance and essential goodness and/or whose pain and suffering cannot be tolerated. Jealousy and fear fuel a victimization that identifies an individual or group as the source of trouble, as something "other" that needs to be "put in its place." Engaging in a process of violence and humiliation is also a way for those who cannot look in the mirror of the other to feel a little better about themselves.

Often the most precious gifts of the persons being tormented are used as weapons against them. This is the curse of the smart child on the playground, the rich culture of a "foreign" land, and the spiritually gifted. The child must be declared uncool, the culture uncivilized, the speaker of truth heretical. The threat of the gift is too much to endure, the brilliance of an individual or a group too illuminating of one's own deficiencies.

And so Jesus' gifts become the crown of thorns in the hands of the Roman soldiers. The crown, a symbol of royalty, is twisted into an instrument of torture. The mocking of Jesus as "King of the Jews" is humiliating enough in itself, yet the words and actions of Jesus—so revelatory and loving in their reality—are twisted and used against him like the thorns. The circular crown symbolizes completeness and royal dignity. The feigned veneration of Jesus as royalty deepens the pain and humiliation. Jesus is tormented for being true to his own identity.

Jesus' greatest crime was not being the Messiah he was expected to be. Every action and word of Jesus proclaimed a reign of God quite different from the power of the world—and the expected power of the Messiah. Jesus was not the king that people were looking for; his revelation of a loving God of justice was simply too threatening to accept. The liberating Word demands a response that is both wondrous and terrifying.

Jesus is silent through the humiliation and pain of the crowning with thorns. As in his encounter with Pilate, Jesus' silence demonstrates the depth of his identity and integrity. Jesus reveals his strength in knowing when to speak and when to stay silent. He does not dignify the twisted definitions or the twisted thorns by accepting them as the only truth. In the midst of persecution, Jesus retains a sense of his own truth. His sense of strength infuriates his tormentors, confirms the faith of his followers, and confuses those who are afraid of taking risks. Jesus stands in the midst of people who want to break him and communicates across time the power of his integrity as the son of God.

I would like to create my one crowd in history to soften the reign of God, the power of love, the pervasiveness of sin. I would like to believe that I am not enraged when God fails to act according to my instructions. I prefer to think that I am not hardened in my images and expectations of God, people, or life itself. But I know, as surely as the sound of angry children travels over my fence, that when I am very tired, disappointed, or temporarily blinded, the crown of thorns is a perfect image for my desire to maintain control. I also know that when I find my own gifts being used as weapons—either by myself or others—Jesus invites me to overcome the ways of the playground.

If our dignity and identity are rooted in God, the need to diminish the light of others is greatly lessened. When we allow the reign of God to illuminate our distorted perceptions of ourselves, there is an emerging wholeness of vision that welcomes the gifted one among us. The crown of thorns thus becomes a meaningless relic of the need to destroy goodness that is troubling. Then, as Jesus promised, we inherit the reign of God.

CARRYING THE CROSS

On their way out, they came across a man from Cyrene,
called Simon, and enlisted him to carry his cross.
(Matthew 27:32)

A late spring snowstorm had blanketed the ground
and formed white clusters on the azalea blossoms. The
contrasts and the contradictions were beautiful, in their
own confusing way.

Plans to plant flowers and make repairs were set
aside for the sake of staying warm and away from a
wind that pierced springtime expectations. Consciousness shifted from the blossoming hints of Easter to out-
of-season chills that put my thoughts squarely back in
the Lent we were still observing.

There was nothing to do that Sunday but respect
the shift in seasons. I took advantage of the unexpected
quiet by visiting a nearby chapel. Appropriate to the
Lenten season, the chapel had on display a series of wa-
tercolors on the theme of the carrying of the cross. The

subject of the series was the Irish potato famine. Although I am of Irish-American descent, I have only recently begun to understand how the trauma of the famine shaped the Irish soul.

What at first glance seems like a faraway tragedy is quite present in its power to speak the truth of carrying the cross. The great tragedy of the Irish famine is, of course, that starvation occurred mainly because of human sin that compounded and magnified the natural disaster of the blight. Decisions were made that affected the supply of food, lands were grabbed, children were taken away from parents, and the worst types of human greed ran rampant across the stricken—and occupied—land. The exhibit I visited during the spring storm is part of a movement to give voice and image to the famine and its legacy.

One of the paintings in the exhibit still haunts me. The image depicted a man who had dug his hand into the ground in hope of finding a small potato. Instead, what he pulled out of the ground was slimy soil afflicted by the blight. There would be no potatoes again that year. The slime pooled on the man's palm and dripped onto the ground. It looked like the stigmata. Marked with the suffering of his people, the man's hand seemed to carry in its shattered hope the very memory of Christ's condemnation, suffering, and death.

That image touched my soul. I felt pressed into service to carry the cross of living memory. Claiming the suffering of my own people was a way of accepting the crossbeam of the profound suffering of all peoples.

Certainly the Irish famine of the nineteenth century was far from the last great hunger that the earth has known. Currently there is famine in many parts of the globe because of natural disasters and bad human decisions. The shackles of international financial practices bind many of the world's people to a poverty that starves with the cruelty of the Great Hunger. Violence between peoples compounds hunger and magnifies the casualties, as in the Balkans. The people of God carry the stigmata in their hunger and their longing for peace, the suffering no less compelling when their ancestry does not match my own.

To become conscious of the cross being carried by others is to be changed in one's view of life. Having seen malnourished children face-to-face, I am unable able to look at an egg, a bowl of rice, or the crops in a field without reverence. This is not a sentimental thing; it is consciousness that calls for conversion. Metanoia is deepened in finding that the reign of God is inhabited by the brokenhearted. To be grief-stricken is to understand that the carrying of the cross is an immediate and active endeavor that extends beyond the suffering of one individual. It is to feel the pain of the hungry, and then to feed them.

The carrying of the cross presses our lives into service appropriate for an ever-shifting awareness of where

God meets us on the road. We are called to notice and respond when the way of the cross merges with paths of our own making and changes the journey abruptly, as does an unexpected storm.

Confusing though it may be, there is a stark promise beneath the weight of the cross. Often we experience the change and its promise in the concrete reality of our own lives. The crossbeams of illness, sudden death, hopelessness, unabated grief, and incomplete understandings are familiar upon our shoulders. Broken relationships and hope turned to affliction weigh down our hearts.

To become conscious of the cross we carry, as well as to be moved by the cross of others, is to become connected to the action of God through the community. Life demands that we both carry the cross and help others to do the same. There is a holy solidarity experienced in the reality that carrying others' burdens lessens and deepens the meaning of our own.

The gospel accounts of Jesus carrying the cross make clear that the crossbeam was placed upon shoulders already weakened and tired. Jesus on the road to Calvary is exhausted. He is vulnerable, like we are so often already weakened and vulnerable when burdens are placed upon us. Jesus is not preaching in this moment of defenselessness. He is overcome by the power of the ordeal and, by necessity, there is a surrender of will, control, and perhaps awareness itself.

There are moments in life when exhaustion and pain are their own type of consciousness. There is no poetry in the struggle to survive hunger or the living consciousness of a tired body in pain. It is difficult for those who are strong to willingly enter that kind of consciousness and its resulting dependency. It is perhaps even more difficult to imagine that this is somehow the path where God is revealed.

Because of Jesus' vulnerability and exhaustion, Simon is pulled from the road to assist Jesus. A new revelation begins as Jesus surrenders to Simon's aid. Vulnerability yields to strength as strength walks with the broken. God is present in the new communion. It is unlikely that Simon had an opportunity to refuse his role in the carrying of the cross. His task is difficult and the timing not of Simon's choosing. However, tradition indicates that Simon was so moved by the experience of helping Jesus to carry the cross that he became a great disciple of Jesus. Simon subsequently carried the news of the resurrection and became well known in the surrounding Christian communities.

How true his experience is to our own. We are, at various times in our lives, both Jesus and Simon of Cyrene. We are sometimes pressed into service as both compassionate witness and carrier of the cross. Life draws us into the way of the cross, perhaps unwillingly accepted at first, and so unifies our individual experience of suffering with that of all God's people. None of us is meant to carry the cross in isolation. Jesus drew from the strength of community.

The living reality is that the way of the cross is present in our lives constantly. The consciousness of conversion invites us to surrender the crossbeam when we are vulnerable and to carry it for others when the living memory of God moves us to compassion. The other option is to be bound by decisions that turn fertile soil into a place of death. The choice for conversion is as continuous as history itself.

THE CRUCIFIXION

"My God, my God, why have you forsaken me?"
(Mark 15:34)

There is a great temptation to try and explain away the crucifixion of Jesus. From the vantage point of those whose lives have known resurrection, the cross can be set aside as something that "happened on the way" to the empty tomb. The harshness of the cross, the agony of Jesus' death, the mystery of suffering, the humiliation of God's own son—these are difficult things to think about, let alone comprehend.

The horror of the cross is compounded by the reality that the son of God, the Prince of Peace, the Wonderful Counselor was executed in a manner generally reserved for criminals and slaves. The flesh of God's own Word was subjected to a cruel death that was both organized and common.

It is easy for me to forgive the disciples of Jesus who ran for their lives rather than standing firm and bearing

witness. All hopes for courage notwithstanding, I am not so sure that I wouldn't have done the same thing myself. In fact, I *have* done the same thing myself.

My capacity to negate the fact that something horrifying was happening, my ability to gather up my fears and walk away, was terribly apparent to me recently. I was rushing home from New York City on a Friday afternoon. Totally exhausted, I was feeling very guarded as I stepped off the subway at the Times Square Station. There was a crowd inconveniently gathered at the bottom of the stairs. As I moved closer to the crowd, I realized that people had gathered around the dead body of a homeless man. Two transit cops were present and a compassionate woman was protecting the dead man's dignity by shielding his face.

A man trying to exit from the first subway door, which was blocked by the crowd, pushed one of the cops aside and stepped over the body. The policeman was furious and said, "What's wrong with you, stepping over a body like it's nothing? Don't you have any respect for the dead?" The man made no reply.

I respected the body enough to walk around it, to try not to stare, and to go up the steps as quickly as possible. I began to think about the horrors of someone dropping dead alone in the Times Square Station, and of the reality of homeless people hidden from view. I wondered about the man's history and what had killed him. Was it his heart? Alcoholism? Lack of medical care? Indifference and abandonment by society? The man on the platform had been a nuisance to the strong when he was alive, and he remained a nuisance in his death. I briefly thought of the observation that civilizations are judged by how they treat their weakest members and I made a harsh judgment of society and of myself.

And then, in my heart and in my body, I walked away from the entire scene. There was a simple reason. I did not care to ponder the next question: Where had God been throughout this man's difficult life and at the moment of his lonely death?

There is nothing more disturbing than to hear or to speak the words "My God, my God, why have you forsaken me?" The feeling of abandonment by God is one of total devastation. Can there be a deeper despair than that evoked by the sense that our loving God either does not care or, worse still, has willingly looked away from human suffering?

The cry of the psalmist "Where is our God now?" is a song, and a sign of the cross. Looking away may be momentarily helpful but, in the end, the reality and the disturbance of the cross cannot be escaped. We live it far too often for that to be possible.

Jesus' death on the cross holds within it the deepest wounds of human life. Jesus experienced the betrayal and cowardice of intimate friends. He experienced religious hostility, state-organized torture, the loss of his life's work, and overwhelming physical pain. He knew in his wounds the sin of the world. Jesus took upon himself the suffering of all of humanity, the sin and the abandonment, the desperation and the dreadful ways that human beings find to torture each other.

The Talmud records that, at the time of Jesus, it was a common practice for compassionate Jews to offer crucifixion victims a bitter mixture of wine and gall as a narcotic to numb their pain. This act of mercy is depicted in the gospel of Matthew. In that narrative, Jesus accepts the compassion by tasting the mixture, but he does not drink it. Jesus' refusal of the numbing wine is a choice to remain conscious in his suffering, to experience, with full awareness, every element of it, including the sense of total abandonment.

The cross is sin and suffering in the raw, before the resurrection, before there is wholeness of understanding. The meaning of the cross becomes abundantly clear in our lives the first time we are naked in the face of its raw suffering. When we experience or stand witness to a suffering for which the only appropriate words are "My God, my God, why have you forsaken me?" the meeting of God and humanity on the cross lose abstraction.

That intimate connection can be found in human suffering across the globe and in the privacy of our own personal suffering. When we experience the cross in our lives, remaining conscious of the pain is a vital link to the presence of the God who joined humanity. Through the cross, we are drawn into the consciousness of God: love present in unimaginable suffering.

Everything about the life and suffering of Jesus transcends the usual boundaries and categories. As in the time of Jesus, so too in our own experience, God does not reveal everything at once. Rather, the meaning unfolds with the joys and sorrows of human life. We discover that God is with us both in desperation and in transcendence. We are invited to a consciousness that experiences not only pain, but also the presence of God in moments of powerlessness.

Jesus passes through the experience of abandonment to a moment of surrender in faith. Jesus turns to the very God who seems absent to experience comfort and peace. Such is the paradox of being conscious: while the horror of God's possible abandonment looms large, we must turn to God in hope. That longing of our spirit is confirmation of God's presence. At the moment when we cannot directly see God, we are held by a deep love that longs to bring us into unity with the flesh of the cross.

Jesus' surrender to the deeper love gives us hope beyond familiar standards. Our cries of abandonment are, in fact, the longing of our hearts to experience new communion.

Standing at the foot of the cross has historically been considered one of the seven sorrows of Mary. She stood witness to the pain and death of the child she had miraculously borne. Mary stood firm while others faltered in their faith. As at the moment of annunciation, we are not to assume that Mary knew with certainty how this story would end. Yet she remained faithful in her belief that with God all things are possible and, among those possibilities, was divine presence in the face of the cross. We see in that unbroken relationship the power of conscious witness.

In our raw sorrows, the meaning of God's presence is revealed in depths we could not have previously imagined. Our calling is to bear witness and trust the very God whose presence seems tenuous. There we will surely know that great sorrow has pierced God's flesh and made us one. Raw though that truth may be, it is the ground beneath feet that do not run away.

It is Emmanuel.

The Glorious Mysteries

THE RESURRECTION

Filled with awe and great joy,
the women came quickly away from the tomb
and ran to tell his disciples.
(Matthew 28:8)

My husband's life abruptly began ten weeks prematurely. Dick was such a tiny baby that the nurses baptized him while the doctor was wondering out loud whether his digestive tract was developed enough to handle nourishment. Because his lungs were vulnerable, there was no time to worry about his nutritional needs. Dick's life was saved because he was put into an incubator filled with 100 percent oxygen.

Dick was in his mid-thirties when he discovered that the miracle of his life carried scars. Too much pure oxygen in the incubator had caused his retinas to develop a dangerous pattern of attachment. This was discovered on a rainy morning in March when Dick woke up blinded by a hemorrhage in one eye.

When Dick's retina detached, it did so quietly. Because the hemorrhage had already robbed him of sight, Dick had no way of knowing that, physiologically, his eye could not see. The detached retina was discovered by the ophthalmologist during a follow-up visit for the hemorrhage.

Surgery was performed the next day to reattach the retina in Dick's left eye. A laser treatment was also done to strengthen the retina in his right eye in the hope of reducing the risk of a future detachment. As the healing progressed, it became apparent that this strengthened, yet vulnerable, eye had become the clearest source of sight. The scars in the other eye ran deep; tiny, nourishing blood vessels had died before the surgery and could not be restored. Although the retina had been reattached, Dick's vision in that eye was badly damaged. Eventually we were told that the wounded sight was the best that could be expected. We were also warned that, as a result of the surgery, cataracts might develop in the future.

Our perspectives were changed by the ophthalmologist's words. As Dick recovered, vulnerability became familiar and future plans were adjusted to a new reality. And, with his changed eyes, Dick looked at the world through the miracle's scars.

Nine years later, a cataract developed on Dick's left eye. Surgery done by a skilled ophthalmologist with expertise in the eye problems of premature babies—even premature babies in their forties—removed the cataract.

Dick healed quickly. However, he was told that there was a cataract forming in his right eye and that he might have to go through a period of functional blindness while the cataract ripened.

A few years later, that cataract developed so quickly that from a Friday to a Monday, Dick lost the ability to read his office computer screen. The swift growth of the cataract was catastrophic. Initially told by his ophthalmologist that surgery was too risky given the underlying retina condition, Dick had the sinking feeling that he was being asked to protect his retina by surrendering his sight.

The difficulty of getting through each day taxed his energy. He bought a magnifying glass and held papers and the glass very close to his eye. With great effort, he took his final exam in a graduate course at New York University. The logic of waiting as long as possible to correct the cataract became harder and harder to accept.

Dick made the decision to seek a second opinion from the surgeon who had done his initial retina surgery. That surgeon was at the University of Iowa, while we were in New York. We had no certainty that insurance would cover the doctor's fees, and we needed to arrange care for our children.

All of these logistical problems were solved within twenty-four hours of our families' learning about Dick's situation. My sister Ann arranged the appointments at the university; my brother Nick provided plane tickets.

Dick's sister Rose flew her grown son from Seattle to New York to care for our children. All of this was done in a spirit of love that said, "This is what brothers and sisters do for each other." We were grateful beyond words, and no words were asked of us.

It was a quick trip with profound meaning. We were met at the airport by Ann who loaned us her car for the ninety-mile drive to see Dick's parents. The next day, we made our way to the University of Iowa Hospitals just as the spring morning was most tender.

The fog lingering over the freshly planted fields and the tiny prairie flowers were so beautiful that tears welled up in my eyes. Those tears lingered longer with the realization that Dick could not see the beauty that I saw; at this moment, his vision of prairie flowers and Iowa mornings was based more on memory than on direct sight.

The doctor remembered Dick and the complications of his case. After looking carefully at Dick's eyes, the man whom Dick most trusted with his eyes told him that it was quite possible for him to see clearly again. "Go back to New York," said Dr. Weingeist, "and have the surgery. It is clearly worth the risk."

So it was that I came to be in the waiting room of a New York City hospital while my husband was in a surgical suite on the other side of an impenetrable wall. I went into an empty space as I waited, reading without comprehending, feeling great restlessness without leaving the chair, looking at the clock without understanding time.

Eventually, Dick's doctor came into the room and told me that everything had gone well. He also told me that he had underestimated the cataract; it was as if my husband had been trying to see through thick, amber-hued glass. The retina had stayed in place but the doctor urged caution in the days ahead.

Less than twenty-four hours later, Dick's vision had changed from functional blindness to 20/20. The lens implanted after removal of the cataract corrected Dick's astigmatism and gave him the best sight he had ever had in his life. From the blurry, frightening space, from the empty place of waiting, from the hours in the tomb came the brightness of new vision.

It was early June and the world was clothed in the colors of rebirth. As we walked to the parking garage, Dick took it all in. "I can see again," he said, "I can see." It was a beautiful day to see again.

And thus sight was renewed and made holy, each petal more precious, each smile more treasured, each remembered vision a harbinger of hope. The scar of one miracle gave way to a new and clearer sight. The tomb was empty.

Experiences of death and resurrection, miracles and transformation, are not always as dramatic as Dick's eye surgery. Yet the elements are clearly present in daily life. We all know something about scars that draw us toward darkness, loss of faith, and hopelessness. The experience of suffering can become a silent scar blinding us to new possibilities and to love.

The resurrection allows us to live with the reality that our lives are filled with both scars and transforming miracles. It teaches us that love is worth the risks. The women who went to the tomb to anoint Jesus' body had vision scarred by the events of the crucifixion. They carried their sadness and vulnerability. Yet, because of their fidelity, they were the first witnesses of the resurrection. In the wonder of love's transformation, they could see the Risen Christ.

Through our brothers and sisters, we meet and reveal the resurrection in love beyond the boundaries of common sight. Therein lies the miracle and the gift of holy sight, of love beyond the scars, of visions of the reign of God well worth the risk.

THE ASCENSION

"And look, I am with you always;
yes, to the end of time."
(*Matthew 28:20*)

Beautiful autumn leaves had fallen and gathered at the base of a stone Celtic cross. The graves of Irish immigrants were clustered around that cross, long ago cemented into the New England ground. Many of the dates of birth were from the dark years when famine sent the Irish to America in the coffin ships. The passage was as threatening as starvation itself. Many children of the famine lived well into their seventies and eighties. Beneath the name and dates of birth and death of one man, this sentence was chiseled into the stone: "*Leave the ashes, take the fire.*"

Within those few words are a philosophy of life and a statement of faith experience. When surrounded by ruins and remains, it is remarkably easy to forget about the spark of life waiting to be reignited. During times of

challenge, change, and threat, the finality of the ashes can be quite seductive. The temptation to obsessively mourn the old way of knowing precludes hope and rebirth.

Yet, at some moment in time, even the ashes must be left behind so that a new fire can be kindled. The difficulty lies in the reality that there is usually an "in-between" time, a time of waiting. Letting go of one reality before the new one is clear is always a test of knowing where to look for God. Most commonly, we look toward what we know, which may be in the ashes, or in the last place we felt certain in our faith. God, in fact, may not be found in either familiar place.

In the mystery of the ascension, Jesus returns to the eternal presence of God. The ascension makes perfect sense in terms of the biblical tradition and Jesus' identity as the Son of God. Biblically, ascension into heaven happens to the holy ones and prophets, such as Enoch and Elijah. The ascension and promise of the Spirit place Jesus and his human experience at the heart of God. The richness of the Trinity unfolds more deeply from the time of the ascension forward.

At the moment of ascension, however, the Spirit has not yet been sent to Jesus' followers. They have been instructed to go to Jerusalem and wait for the Spirit. This time of waiting places Jesus' friends in the moment between ashes and fire. They must not stay too long in the ashes of fear and uncertainty. At the same time, Jesus' followers must rely on their experience of the loving fire to direct them in their search to know him in a new way.

This tension is reflected in an image and a question that appears both in the gospel of Luke and the Acts of the Apostles. The image is that of Jesus' friends and followers looking for him in the last place they saw him, unaware that a great transformation has taken place. The question comes through an angel or witness who simply asks "Why are you looking for Christ in the ashes?" Luke's gospel tells the story of the women going to the tomb of Jesus and finding it empty. Reminded of Jesus' words by the brilliantly dressed men, the women realize that Jesus has fulfilled his promises and risen from the dead.

The gospel of Luke goes on to describe what must have been an idyllic time. Jesus' friends recognize him in the breaking of the bread and his greetings of peace. They are comforted by the Risen Jesus and find new intimacy with him. The painful events of the passion are brought into wholeness during these days after the resurrection. The followers of Jesus know that he is not to be found among the dead—he is risen and with them.

The Acts of the Apostles begins with Jesus instructing the disciples about the gift of the Holy Spirit that they will receive soon. However, as Jesus has said from the beginning, it is necessary that he depart from them so that the Spirit might be given to them. There is little time between the final instructions and the moment when Jesus ascends into heaven. The disciples are caught by surprise and stand looking upward, expecting to find Jesus where they last saw him—among the clouds. For the second time, Jesus' friends are not sure where he is.

As they wonder, two men walk by and ask them why they are looking for Jesus in the sky. Were the disciples not listening when Jesus explained about returning to heaven and sending the Spirit? Didn't they understand that he would ascend to God so that his Spirit could be sent to them?

It is doubtful that the disciples fully understood everything that Jesus had told them, because the glory of God is too much for human beings to grasp all at once. They had to rely on the pain and glory that had already been revealed to them before they could receive the full meaning of the ascension.

Deep within, I know the moment. It is hard to re-member the teachings and experience of the past when, in a particular experience, Jesus suddenly seems absent. When my arthritis pain abates in a moment of mercy, I am full of knowledge of wholeness and the Risen Jesus. It is easy then; the resurrection and ascension feel pre-sent in my flesh. When the pain returns, and it always does, there is a transitional moment when I do not know how to pray or where to look for God. It is as if the Jesus I was praising has suddenly vanished into the clouds, dis-tant from the concerns of my wounded feet. The fulfill-ment of the prophecies is far from my mind when I am not quite sure what to do with myself while painfully waiting for the promised Pentecost to come. The mystery of the ascension and Jesus' return to God temporarily breaks the intimate connection with Jesus as I knew it in the time of resurrection.

At such times, I find it difficult to believe that the emptiness of physical pain and what sometimes feels like sudden departure is the prelude to a deeper experience of God. Thus I find that I am often looking at the sky when the experience of Jesus is to be found on the ground, heaven and earth joined in the human experience of living in hope. For something deeper is, in fact, born when Jesus ascends to heaven. I do not always fully understand it, but, nonetheless, the promise of life is more powerful than doubt.

The mystery of the ascension flows from the mystery of the resurrection. Taken together, these mysteries are living reminders of the truth that the times of confusion, of emptiness and longing, are meant to yield to a newness of life and unity with God. Jesus' return to God takes the moment of loss of certainty about how to pray or where to look for God and transforms it into preparation for the fire and wind of Pentecost.

Searching for God in the wrong places—including my linking of Jesus' presence to an absence of pain—is ended by the experience and promise of fire. Jesus is with us to the end of time in a unity beyond telling; heaven to earth, earth to heaven, a transforming fire of love.

THE SENDING OF THE HOLY SPIRIT

From this time, they were all filled with the Holy Spirit and
began to proclaim the word of God fearlessly.
(Acts 4:31)

There are times in life when the Holy Spirit is experienced as a great, dramatic gust of wind that transforms human fear into fire. Those are the powerful moments when unexpected conversion happens and chaos makes way for communion. Scripture and the writings of the saints tell eloquently of such visitations of the Spirit. It is at the moment of Pentecost when disciples of Christ are empowered to know him in their midst, and to proclaim the gospel without fear.

Most of us have known—perhaps in retrospect—moments of presence and transformation so powerful that the Spirit of God was obviously present. Yet most of my own experiences with the Holy Spirit are more subtle, like a Pentecost that slips into daily life. While there are actions of the Spirit as dramatic as a mighty wind, the Spirit's presence with us is the breath of life.

Biblically, breath is a metaphor for the Spirit of God. Breath and spirit are, in fact, the same word in Hebrew, Latin, and Greek. Breath, though invisible, goes to the innermost part of the human being. Breath is the life force, the dwelling place, the carrier of God. To draw in breath is to be in God's presence. Breath is the spirit that gives life. In the book of Genesis, God creates living beings by sharing breath. Wisdom is called "breath of the living God." In the gospel of John, the Risen Jesus breathes on his disciples, saying, "Receive the Holy Spirit." And in the Acts of the Apostles, that Spirit graces the earth in a great, transforming breath of wind. With that breath comes *inspiration* and understanding, the Spirit drawn in as an enlivening, healing force.

It is easy to live without consciousness of our breath until it is threatened in some way. Just as we sometimes physically stop and catch our breath, awareness of the Spirit among us requires conscious attention. I have come to believe that one sign of God's constant presence are the breath marks in life that invite me to pause and give thanks for the dwelling of the Spirit in my body and soul.

Breath marks in music are tiny commas above the staff that give the song a steady flow of life. They are the pauses that allow for interpretation and expression of the composer's meaning. I am startled to discover breath marks within the ordinary notes of my life, so many revitalizing reminders to let God's breath, God's Spirit, mingle with my own. Breath marks are experiences in my tactile daily life—dishes in the sink, heart filled with good intentions, body tired and grumpy— that let me know that God's energy is, indeed, as close as breath. Breath marks are encounters with life in small slices that result in renewal of faith. They are moments when perspective changes and it is possible to speak in the tongues of compassion.

One such breath mark is a small jar of yeast that I keep in my refrigerator, long past its expiration date. My mother brought the yeast with her when she and my in-laws traveled twelve hundred miles for my son's first communion. I had asked my mother if she would make rolls for the party, and she happily agreed. Uncertain about whether or not she could find the right yeast in New York, she brought along the jar, confident that, with this particular leaven, her rolls would rise.

It happened that I had had surgery a few days before the first communion celebration. While the procedure itself had gone well, it exhausted me in a way that I had not anticipated. When the mothers arrived, I was given a space to rest and heal. They tended to the cooking and the laundry and the immediate needs of my children. They gently and firmly sent me out of the kitchen and prepared the first communion meal. Central to that meal were the rolls my mother kneaded. The strength of her hands, the recipe known by heart, the consistency of her care, the power of her love brought the yeast to life. And the rolls did rise.

We had a grand celebration of Patrick's first communion. Friends joined us to eat the rolls and continue the eucharistic meal, pictures were taken, memories were made. By the time the grandparents left, I felt much stronger. The yeast left behind in the refrigerator became a powerful breath mark. Each time I reached for it, I caught my breath. I remembered the surgery, the celebration, the love between a mother and a child. In the course of that remembering, the significance of feeding my children turned the dreaded kitchen tasks into a marker of the circle of life.

There are breath marks all around us. They are unexpected gifts in the course of the day, gifts that renew the tired heart—like a smile from the most cantankerous of my neighbors just as I am about to judge her sorrow harshly. The need to pause and breathe in that Spirit of God usually does not arise in moments of clarity and apparent strength. Rather, the breath mark often catches me in moments of mistaken self-reliance or the snare of pride. Those sins are the ones that would make me think that my particular sorrows, understandings of life, and challenges are justification for alienation instead of opportunities to be open to and understand a different language.

At such moments, I deeply long for conversion in the small spaces of my life where love is constricted, wonders are ignored, growth is suppressed. The gospels remind us that small things reveal the reign of God—sheep tended lovingly, lamp wicks trimmed wisely, a woman looking everywhere for the lost coin. Is it not the revelation of God in such tiny breath marks that made the message of the parables unacceptable for so many?

Responding to the deeper meaning of the breath marks requires a discipline that actualizes one of the fundamental truths of our received religious wisdom: spirituality requires practices to express and nourish it. To approach life reverently, pausing often to rest and receive the breath of life, reframes consciousness in the certain knowledge that God's generosity is boundless. We gain the discipline of that consciousness not in one great inhalation that lasts a lifetime, but in responding to the need—over and over again—to pause and accept the gracious and transforming energy of God.

Guarding the heart's capacity for gratitude and joy—regardless of circumstances that would pull us toward grief—is possible when the scriptural call to pray without ceasing is drawn into one's body and held there as a source of life. I am called by God to train my sight on those ordinary moments of recollection and renewal. The sending of the Holy Spirit is as present as the breath marks, and breath, of life.

THE ASSUMPTION OF MARY INTO HEAVEN

Seeing his mother and the disciple whom he loved standing near her, Jesus said to his mother, "Woman, this is your son." Then to the disciple he said, "This is your mother."
(John 19:26-27)

Recently I read a compilation of oral histories of women who had faced the horror of losing a child. The poignancy of the narratives was deepened by the fact that the women told the stories as if the events had happened moments earlier, even though in some cases the stories being told were more than half a century old.

Living memory becomes ordinary when traumatic life events bind their images to the human soul in a way that transcends time. For mothers and fathers who have had to bury their children, time and memory become inextricably linked with a terrible knowledge of pain. It is difficult to trust life—or God—after a child has died. And yet, there are brave souls who dare to live again after such a grievous experience, who dare to trust again,

who dare to believe even as the memory of pain remains deeply present to them.

It is always an awesome thing to multiply the pain and courage of individual experience across the globe and the centuries. When considering the premature death of children, the magnitude of suffering is immeasurable. Because of modern technology and mass media, we have an increased awareness of the children—and parents—lost to war, famine, AIDS, the Holocaust, poverty, and other disasters. During the past hundred years, cameras have witnessed the excavation of mass graves all over the world. Some images linger in our collective consciousness with the power of traumatic memory: My Lai, the Auschwitz burial pits, the bodies in Rwanda. Behind each image is the suffering of a mother, a father, and a child that bonds to the soul and retains immediacy.

Mary, the mother of Jesus, experienced that profound suffering. Perhaps nowhere was her suffering more apparent than at the foot of the cross. When the pain of the world, its sin and its suffering, were breaking Mary's heart, Jesus gave her to John—and to us—as Mother. She who had borne the most desperate of human losses was one of the first witnesses to the resurrection. The Acts of the Apostles reports that Mary was with the disciples in Jerusalem when the Church was born. Tradition teaches that Mary stayed in Jerusalem until she departed with St. John to lead a Christian community in Ephesus. Mary was a leading figure in the early days of the Church as the Mother of God, the Mother of the Church, and the Mother of all believers.

Mary's courage allowed her to see the Risen Jesus and, indeed, to become mother to the world. Mary carried in her body the immediacy of human suffering and the experience of grace that consecrates—and ultimately redeems—the whole person. The fruit of Mary's womb is the Savior. She whose body gave physical form to Jesus understands well the struggles of life and death. As the Mother of God and of humanity, Mary knows that the redemption of the human soul is intimately connected with the experience and suffering of the body.

So it is that we pray and celebrate the mystery of Mary's assumption into heaven, body and soul. The essential human experiences that mark her life are taken into heaven in her earthly form. That Mary, in her historical being and personality, is assumed into heaven after death further reveals the creation of a new heaven and a new earth. The world and God are not what we previously thought them to be. The life, death, and resurrection of Christ initiate a new order not dependent on a tyranny of the powerful. Mary's assumption embodies and represents the destination of all redeemed in Christ.

In the struggle between life and death, the powerful forces of evil and sin do not have the last word. The power of God will prevail, even in the most overwhelming circumstances. The physical immediacy of Mary's experience, memory, and grace are taken into heaven as a living witness to a power that liberates rather than condemns. Mary, full of grace, exemplifies the action of God in human life. Her assumption into heaven gives glory to her nearness to God as the source of all life and love.

How powerful the mystery of the assumption becomes when we let ourselves become aware of the devaluation of human life and the enormous suffering brought about by human decisions and sin. The assumption mystery that our bodies and souls are both works of God, redeemed by God, and received by God in the resurrection restores dignity and upholds our true identity as children of God. The assumption of Mary is a proclamation and demonstration of faith that leads to greater understanding of how we are all connected in God. From that understanding comes a deeper care for our brothers and sisters.

Mary's assumption brings the journey of life, death, faith and care of others to our bodies in both an immanent and a transcendent way. To proclaim Mary's fullness of life—on earth and in heaven—is to assert that the life journey is holy.

The memory of Mary's assumption has an immediacy that reaches out and bonds itself to our souls, not because of the trauma she endured, but because of the total communion she lives in God's presence. That presence is a grace in our own lives, the Spirit of God crossing the barriers of time and space, drawing us into a new knowledge of who we really are.

MARY CROWNED QUEEN OF HEAVEN AND EARTH

"Of all women, you are the most blessed,
and blessed is the fruit of your womb."
(Luke 1:42)

Shinyanga is located in northern Tanzania, East Africa. It is a small rural town with few streets, most of them unpaved. It is not what would be called a pretty town and is, in fact, a somewhat raffish "cow town" reminiscent of the Old West. It is on a rail line between the coastal capital, Dar es Salaam, and the large town of Mwana, on Lake Victoria. Shinyanga is the main center of commerce for the people of the surrounding countryside.

The majority of the Sukuma people in the region are agricultural. They generally live in simple, mud-brick houses with grass roofs. Whatever they have of value, whether it is a small crop of cotton, a cow, a goat, or surplus rice, is taken to town and sold to meet more pressing needs, such as medicine or clothing.

Due to changing weather patterns over the last few years, Shinyanga and the surrounding area have seen more than their share of natural disasters and extreme weather conditions. During the 1990s, East Africa in general suffered droughts, floods, crop loss, and the resultant economic disaster that made life difficult even at the most basic level. Those who lived on the fringes of the town had little money available for food, school fees, clothing, or rent.

To obtain money for basic needs, the women of Shinyanga had to do exhausting work, such as sifting rice husks for the meager kernels they contain. If no work was available, they were reduced to begging for assistance at the local parish.

While providing direct monetary assistance on a case-by-case basis offered immediate relief, everyone realized that it was not a helpful long-term strategy. Something different was needed in Shinyanga, and the droughts of the 1990s called for new and creative alternatives that would promote self-reliance for the women of the area.

A fortunate resource found in the Shinyanga area are the beautiful seeds on the trees, flowers, and vines. The seeds are small, hard, uniform, and readily available. During the hardest of times, the beauty of the seeds begged to be material in the hands of the women. Surely, with their gifts, the women could make them into something valuable.

The mothers of Shinyanga found financial assistance and independence by taking the seeds and making them into prayer beads that mark the mysteries in the lives of Jesus and his mother. From the needs, the seeds, the gifts of the women, the leadership of Christina, an African woman from across Lake Victoria, the inspiration of a missionary priest, and the blessings of the Holy Spirit, a rosary workshop was born in Buhangija Parish.

It took time and experimentation to figure out the best way to make the rosaries. The seeds are small and working with them requires great care and intensive labor. They must be hand sanded on each side so that a sixteenth-of-an-inch drill bit can make a hole through them. Without the hole, there can be no rosary. A rosary has fifty-nine beads, each of which must go through the delicate preparation process. The work takes time.

Sometimes the women take the seeds home and sand them while watching their children. Sometimes the sanding is done by groups of women. The prepared seeds are then carefully carried to the workshop where they are divided by color, size, and eventually decades of prayer.

Once the holes are drilled, the seeds are carefully strung together on wire or cord from Our Lady's Rosary Makers in Louisville, Kentucky. The materials find their way to Africa in different ways and through different hands. Sometimes the material is hand carried by a single traveler. Sometimes it passes through dozens of hands in a shipping process. The crucifix at the end of the rosary comes from a small shop around the corner from St. Peter's Square in Rome. The rosary made from the seeds of Shinyanga holds within itself pieces of three continents. The disparate pieces are made one in the careful hands of women whose love for their families becomes an art of prayer.

The rosary beads made in the Urembo Workshop are sold in Tanzania and abroad. They have sold well, because the rosary beads are strong and beautiful, much like the women who make them. The women have suffered hardship and sorrow. They have stood at the foot of the cross with tremendous consciousness of what is happening. Their love and their art reflect great courage in the face of pain and hardship. The rosary beads made by these women of conscious love are pieces of heaven and earth, both figuratively and literally.

The women and the rosaries made by them reflect the beauty of Mary, the Queen of Heaven and Earth. She who carried God, gave birth in a stable, treasured her memories, stood at the cross, and witnessed the glory of the resurrection is remembered and glorified in African seeds passing through the hands of all who believe.

Mary's faith, suffering, and perseverance are ever present in our lives. Mary, Queen of Heaven and Earth, reveals our true identity as servants and lovers of God. She brings together the smallest of seeds, the deepest of needs, the breadth of despair and imagination and holds them blessed in the reign of God.

Giving Mary the title of Queen acknowledges her as a woman of wisdom who embodies and understands the interaction between God and humanity. It is she who carried Christ into the world, and now she joins him as Queen of earth and of heaven. The fruit of Mary's womb is the love of Christ which shines like the stars and guides us through droughts and wilderness spaces like the Exodus pillar of fire.

The women of Shinyanga are not the first nor will they be the last people of the earth to encounter drought and hunger. Yet the love and imagination that have allowed the women to provide for their families in the creation of rosary beads fulfills the prophecy of Mary's Magnificat.

> God has pulled down princes from their thrones
> and raised high the lowly.
> God has filled the starving with good things, sent
> the rich away empty. (Luke 1:52-54)

The fulfillment of the reign of God brought to birth by Mary changed heaven and earth forever. Mary is Queen of the angels, prophets, apostles, saints, confessors, the Queen of peace and of the cosmos. She is the Queen of all generations, her presence as near as small seeds, fingers, and memory.

Mary is the Mother of God who prays for us and gently calls us home. Her voice is heard in our hearts each time we long for justice, communion, love, and peace. Hers is the regal presence that echoes the Angel Gabriel's "Do not be afraid." And, with Mary, courage and a new creation is born from the smallest of seeds.

APPENDIX

HOW TO PRAY THE ROSARY

Realizing that there is an entire generation of Catholics who have grown up since the rosary was said regularly in public, I give below simple directions on how the rosary is prayed.

The first and most important thing to remember is that the mysteries of the rosary revolve around many of the primary events in the life of Jesus and that of his mother. The rosary involves memorizing several fundamental prayers and reciting them while meditating on the twenty "mysteries" of the rosary. While many devoted people pray all twenty of the mysteries on a given day (which takes from thirty to forty-five minutes), it is more common to pray five mysteries on any given day (which takes about ten to fifteen minutes).

General practice is to meditate on the "Glorious" mysteries on Sundays, Wednesdays, and solemn feast days;

the "Joyful" mysteries on Mondays and Saturdays; the "Mysteries of Light" on Thursdays; and the "Sorrowful" mysteries on Tuesdays and Fridays.

Method of Reciting the Rosary*

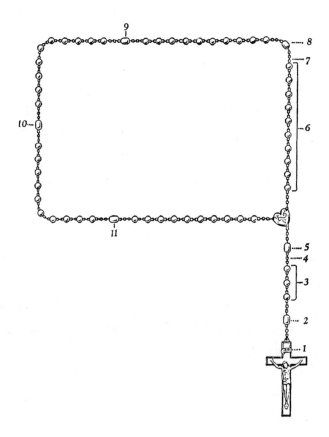

---

*Adapted from Patrick Payton, CSC, *The Ear of God:* (Garden City, N.Y.: Doubleday, 1951), p. 181.

1. Make the Sign of the Cross and Say the Apostles' Creed
2. Say the Our Father
3. Say three Hail Marys
4. Say the Glory Be
5. Announce the first mystery; then say the Our Father
6. Say ten Hail Marys
7. Say the Glory Be
8. Announce the second mystery; then say the Our Father, ten Hail Marys, and one Glory Be
9. Announce the third mystery; then say the Our Father, ten Hail Marys, and one Glory Be
10. Announce the fourth mystery; then say the Our Father, ten Hail Marys, and one Glory Be
11. Announce the fifth mystery; then say the Our Father, ten Hail Marys, and one Glory Be

In many places, when the rosary as described above is finished, either the Hail Holy Queen or the Memorare (composed by Saint Bernard of Clairvaux, 1090-1153) is recited. In some places, it is the custom to recite both.

The Twenty Mysteries of the Rosary

Following are the mysteries (or "decades") of the rosary. I have given chapter and verse reference numbers in the gospels and Acts of the Apostles.

Sometimes, when the rosary is prayed by a group, the leader designates a person in the group to read one of the biblical accounts of a mystery. (This may, of course, be done by an individual praying the rosary alone.)

The Joyful Mysteries

* *The Annunciation* (the Archangel Gabriel tells Mary she is to give birth to Jesus, Luke 1:26-38)
* *The Visitation* (Mary visits her cousin Elizabeth, pregnant with John the Baptist, Luke 1:39-56)
* *The Nativity of Jesus* (Luke 2:1-20; Matthew 1:18–2: 12)
* *The Presentation of Jesus in the Temple* (to fulfill the law dedicating Jesus as the firstborn male to God, Luke 2:22-38)
* *Finding the Child Jesus in the Temple* (Luke 2:41-52)

The Mysteries of Light

* *The Baptism in the Jordan* (Matthew 3:1-17)
* *The Wedding Feast at Cana* (John 2:1-12)
* *Preaching the Kingdom of God* (Luke 6:20-35)
* *The Transfiguration* (Matthew 17:1-20)
* *The Institution of the Eucharist* (Mark 14:22-25)

The Sorrowful Mysteries

* *The Agony in the Garden* (Matthew 26:36-56; Mark 14:32-42)

- *The Scourging at the Pillar* (Matthew 27:15-26)
- *The Crowning with Thorns* (Matthew 27:27-31; Mark: 15:16-20; John 19:1-16)
- *Jesus Carries the Cross* (Matthew 27:32; Mark 15:21; Luke 23:26-32)
- *The Crucifixion and Death of Jesus* (Matthew 27:33-61; Mark 15:22-47; Luke 23:33-56; John 19:17-42)

The Glorious Mysteries

- *The Resurrection of Jesus from the Dead* (Matthew 28:1-15; Mark 16:1-18; Luke 24:1-49; John 20:1-31)
- *The Ascension of Jesus into Heaven* (Matthew 28:16-20; Mark 16:19-20; Luke 24:50-53; Acts 1:6-12)
- *The Sending of the Holy Spirit* (Acts 2:1-41)
- *The Assumption of Mary into Heaven, Body and Soul* (This is an ancient church tradition, but there is no reference to it in the New Testament. It was defined as a truth of the Catholic faith by Pope Pius XII on November 1, 1950.)*
- *The Crowning of Mary, Queen of Heaven and Earth* (This last mystery is an ancient church tradition but, as in the case of the mystery of the assumption, there is no reference to it in the New Testament.)

---

*For an excellent summary of church teaching on Mary, see J. Neuner, S.J., and Jacques Dupuis, S.J., eds., *The Christian Faith: Doctrinal Documents of the Catholic Church*, 5th ed. (Staten Island, N.Y.: Alba House, 1991), chapter 8, "The Mother of the Saviour," pp. 213-27.

Prayers Used in the Rosary

The diagram on page 148 shows a rosary; the listing on page 149 indicates the prayers associated with each of its physical parts. The texts of the prayers used in the rosary are as follows.

The Sign of the Cross

In the name of the Father, the Son, and the Holy Spirit. Amen.

The Apostles' Creed

I believe in God, the Father almighty, Creator of heaven and earth.
I believe in Jesus Christ, his only Son, our Lord.
>He was conceived by the power of the Holy Spirit and born of the virgin Mary.
>He suffered under Pontius Pilate, was crucified, died, and was buried.
>He descended to the dead.
>On the third day, he rose again.
>He ascended into heaven, and is seated at the right hand of the Father.
>He will come again to judge the living and the dead.
I believe in the Holy Spirit, the Lord and giver of Life, the holy catholic church, the communion of saints,

the forgiveness of sins, the resurrection of the body, and life everlasting. Amen.

The Our Father

Our Father, who art in heaven, hallowed be thy name.
Thy kingdom come, thy will be done on earth, as it is in heaven.
Give us this day our daily bread and forgive us our trespasses, as we forgive those who trespass against us.
Lead us not into temptation, but deliver us from evil. Amen.

Hail Mary

Hail Mary, full of grace, the Lord is with thee.
Blessed art thou among women,
and blessed is the fruit of thy womb, Jesus.
Holy Mary, Mother of God, pray for us sinners
now and at the hour of our death. Amen.

Glory Be...

Glory be to the Father, to the Son, and to the Holy Spirit,
As it was in the beginning, is now, and shall be forever. Amen.

Hail Holy Queen

Hail, Holy Queen, Mother of mercy;
hail, our life, our sweetness and our hope.
To thee do we cry, poor banished children of Eve:
to thee do we sigh, mourning and weeping in this vale
of tears.
Turn then, most gracious Advocate, thine eyes of mercy
toward us and,
after this our exile, show unto us the blessed fruit of thy
womb, Jesus.
O clement, O loving, O sweet Virgin Mary.

The Memorare

Remember, O most gracious Virgin Mary
that never was it known
that anyone who fled to your protection,
implored your help,
or sought your intercession
was left unaided.

Inspired by this confidence,
I fly to you O Virgin of virgins, my mother.
To you I come;
before you I stand,
sinful and sorrowful.

O Mother of the Word Incarnate,
despise not my petitions,

but in your mercy, hear and answer me.
Amen.

I have given the traditional language of the Our Father and the Hail Mary, using the Old English "thou" and "thy." Some persons and groups prefer the more modern "you" and "your" in these prayers. In private recitation of the rosary, an individual may use whichever version he or she prefers. In group recitation, while the version used is to some extent a matter of personal taste, the most important principle is the agreement of the group.

ACKNOWLEDGMENTS

First, I thank Penny Sandoval, Maryann Ferrara, and Rodney Swanger for their assistance in helping me in the Maryknoll Photo Archives. I am deeply grateful to the photographers and artists who have given permission for their pictures to be used in this book, as well as to the Maryknoll Fathers and Brothers who own reproduction rights to many of the photos in this book.

In particular, I express gratitude to:
- Brother Andrew Marsalek, M.M. (1) for the picture of the Mexican woman in the mystery of the annunciation and (2) for the picture of a contemporary baptism in the Jordan River in the mystery of Jesus' baptism.
- Brother John Beeching, M.M. (1) for the picture of the two lay missioners—Ellen Cowhey and Diedre Higgins—in the mystery of the visitation; (2) for the photo of a Nile River sailboat used in the mystery of the sending of the Holy Spirit (Pentecost); and (3) for

the photograph of a refugee child in Thailand used in the mystery of the transfiguration.

– Paul D'Arcy for the picture of Our Lady of the Campo in Chile in the mystery of the presentation in the temple.

– Father James Kroeger, M.M. (1) for the picture of a Bangladeshi boy used in the mystery of the finding of Jesus in the temple; (2) for the photo of a sculpture by Nandor Glid at the Yad-Vashem memorial in Israel to the six million Jews killed in the Holocaust used in the mystery of the scourging of Jesus at the pillar; and (3) for the photo of a statue of aboriginal Taiwanese in the Formosan Aboriginal Cultural Village used in the mystery of the ascension.

– Joseph Fedora, M.M., for the picture of a wedding in mainland China used in the mystery of the marriage at Cana.

– Sean Sprague (1) for the picture of the lay minister in Tanzania used in the mystery of the preaching of the kingdom and (2) for the picture of the celebration of the Eucharist in a Tanzanian home used in the mystery of the institution of the Eucharist.

– Charles S. Ngede for the portrait, "Jesus Is Condemned to Death" from the stations of the cross painted by Ngede on the walls of St. Joseph Mukasa Church in Mwanza, Tanzania. A complete set of Ngede's stations may be found in Diana L. Hayes,

Were You There? Stations of the Cross, art by Charles S. Ngede (Maryknoll, N.Y.: Orbis Books, 2000).

– Eric Wheater for the picture of a Nicaraguan peasant carrying the cross used in the mystery of Jesus carrying the cross (courtesy of the Maryknoll Photo Archives).

– Octavio Duran for the picture of the crucifixion statue group used in the mystery of the crucifixion of Jesus.

– Brother John Argauer, M.M. (1) for the image of the sun shining through the trees used in the mystery of the resurrection; and (2) for the photo of the Guatemalan madonna used in the mystery of the assumption of Mary.

I am grateful to Nancy Schreck, O.S.F., who taught me to see the parables in new ways. I thank my husband Dick who makes writing and all other things possible; my children Michael and Patrick who keep my feet on earth. I am grateful for the confidence and support of Bill Burrows and the staff of Orbis Books.